Books by Anne Brennan & Janice Brewi

*Mid-life Psychological and Spiritual Perspectives*

*Mid-life Directions: Praying, Playing—Sources of New Dynamism*

*Passion for Life: Lifelong Psychological and Spiritual Growth*

*Mid-life Spirituality and Jungian Archetypes*
(revised edition of *Celebrate Mid-life*)

The Jung on the Hudson Book Series was instituted by The New York Center for Jungian Studies in 1997. This ongoing series is designed to present books that will be of interest to individuals of all fields, as well as mental health professionals, who are interested in exploring the relevance of the psychology and ideas of C. G. Jung to their personal lives and professional activities.

For more information about the annual Jung on the Hudson seminars, this series, and the New York Center for Jungian Studies contact: Aryeh Maidenbaum, Ph.D., 27 North Chestnut St., Suite 3, New Paltz, NY 12561, telephone (845) 256-0191, fax (845) 256-0196.

For more information about becoming part of this series, contact: Nicolas-Hays, Inc., P. O. Box 1126, Berwick, ME 03901-1126, telephone: (207) 698-1041, fax: (207) 698-1042, e-mail: info@nicolashays.com.

# Mid-life Psychological and Spiritual Perspectives

## Janice Brewi and Anne Brennan

NICOLAS-HAYS, INC.
BERWICK, MAINE

Revised edition published in 2004 by
Nicolas-Hays, Inc.
P.O. Box 1126
Berwick, ME 03901
www.nicolashays.com

**Library of Congress Cataloging in Publication Data**

Brewi, Janice.
    Mid-life—psychological and spiritual perspectives.

    Bibliography: p.
    1. Middle age — Religious life. 2. Middle age—Psychological aspects.
I. Brennan, Anne. II. Title.
BV4579.5.B73                          248.8'4          81-19512
ISBN 0-89254-089-3                    AACR2

Cover art by Delle S. Morris.
Cover design by Kathryn Sky-Peck.
Printed in the United States of America
BJ

| 10 | 09 | 08 | 07 | 06 | 05 | 04 |
|----|----|----|----|----|----|----|
| 7  | 6  | 5  | 4  | 3  | 2  | 1  |

The paper used in this publication meets the minimum requirements of
the American National Standard for Information Sciences—Permanence
of Paper for Printed Library Materials Z39.48–1992 (R1997).

*To*
*Grace and Michael Brewi*
*and*
*Anne and Michael Brennan,*
*Roots in life and in faith*

# Contents

# Acknowledgments

*The Collected Works of C. G. Jung*, ed. by Gerhard Adler, Michael Fordham, Herbert Read and William McGuire, trans. by R. F. C. Hull. Bollingen Series XX. Princeton University Press. Used with gracious permission.

*Memories, Dreams, Reflections*, C. G. Jung, translated by Richard and Clara Winston, recorded and edited by Aniela Jaffe, copyright © 1961, Random House, Inc. Used with permission.

*Modern Man in Search of a Soul*, Carl G. Jung, trans. W. S. Dell and Cary F. Baynes, copyright © 1955, Harcourt, Brace, Jovanovich, Inc. Used with permission.

"Saint Joan" by Bernard Shaw in *Seven Plays*. Courtesy of The Society of Authors on behalf of the Bernard Shaw Estate.

*The Seasons of a Man's Life*, Daniel J. Levinson, Charlotte N. Darrow, Edward B. Klein, Maria H. Levinson, and Braxton McKee, copyright © 1978, Alfred A. Knopf, Inc. Used with permission.

Lyric excerpt of "Sunrise, Sunset," by Sheldon Harnick and Jerry Bock copyright © 1964 (renewed 1992) by Mayerling Productions Ltd. (Administered by K & H Music) and Jerry Bock Enterprises (USA). Reprinted by permission. All rights reserved.

Excerpt from *The Well and the Cathedral* by Ira Progoff, copyright © 1972, Dialogue House. Used with permission.

# Preface

C arl G. Jung said that every mid-life crisis is a spiritual crisis, a crisis of meaning—and that rediscovery of the sacred is the only cure. Jung believed that loss of the sacred is the illness of our times. Since his day (1875–1961) innumerable mid-life men and women have set out to rediscover the sacred in their own lives, in their own psyches, and in the universe. This search for personal spirituality among today's mid-life adults awakens a thirst to become our own unique Self, develop our own unique way of being in the world, develop our full potential, and work for development of the full potential of all the world's citizens. This book is a guide for that journey.

An adult entering mid-life today in this 21st century can expect to live another 30, 40, or 50 years. The last century gifted us with the doubling of our adult life span here in the US and in much of the world. In 1900, life expectancy in the US was 47, but today a forty-seven-year-old man or woman can look forward to another adulthood. This makes it a moral imperative to grow in our understanding of those mid-life and later years.

In touch with this remarkable emerging phenomena twenty years ago, we developed our first workshop on mid-life. We hoped it would promote the personal and spiritual growth of adults at this crucial time in their lives. We drew on decades of adult developmental psychology, the work of C. G. Jung, and our Judeo-Christian spiritual tradition, as well as contemporary insights into spirituality, such as journaling as a spiritual practice, both music meditation and mandala making as evoking the unconscious, centering prayer as facilitating awareness of the Greater Self and the Divine indwelling.

Early on in the Mid-Life Directions workshops we developed and promoted the Long Life Directions workshop. The Long Life Directions workshop fosters the soul making that only a length of years can bring.

xi

Growth throughout the second half of life has become our life work in these twenty years. This book contains the psychology and theology underlying the Mid-Life Directions workshops. Each chapter (we each wrote four) comprises the thought behind the presentations and processes that are the heart and soul of the workshops. Each Mid-Life Directions workshop is interactive and it is our hope that you too will interact with each chapter of this book as you explore your own life story in the past, at the present moment, and live it onward in years yet to come. This new edition has been revised and updated, and even more importantly, the insights here have been tested and confirmed by mid-life women and men around the globe.

When Mid-Life Directions became our full work, our first invitation to bring Mid-Life Directions to another country was from our neighbor, Canada. Soon after, we were invited to Ireland, where we returned annually for ten years. England followed and then there was the Caribbean, Singapore, and Malaysia.

Mid-Life Directions had quickly become an international and an ecumenical organization. Its non-profit (501-c3) status embraced the community at home and the whole world. A common cord had been touched around the globe. Today, the Mid-Life and Long Life Directions Workshops are being offered by women and men in one or more countries on all 6 continents. Professionals have come to the US to be trained by us to present these workshops to the people in other countries: Canada, Ireland, Australia, England, Italy, Malaysia, Singapore, the Philippines, Peru, Jamaica, St. Kitts, Nigeria, Zimbabwe. These professionals have multiplied the number of workshops presented, and have traveled themselves to other places like Panama, Belize, Ghana, Kenya, South Africa, Nepal, and India. With the first edition of this book, a university professor from India visiting the US called us to say that he was using our book in his classes in India. We were stunned. How could our book, our Mid-Life Directions workshop be respected in India? Today we know it is only because of our common humanity and life cycle. Despite all our cultural differences, at the core we are all the same. There is one humanity. People from different cultures and other continents expressing interest in Mid-Life and Long Life Directions Workshops, and even desirous of facilitating them for the people they live and/or work with, reflect the commonality of the journey and magnificent collective unconscious we all share.

While the theological underpinnings of this book are Christian because that is our particular background, they are not fundamentalist and they are open. Others can read and profit. We believe that the theology of all the world's religions must be open to communicating with one another and with the masses of the world's people they are called to serve. People are in search of a spirituality that is inclusive, that promotes respect for all peoples, that enlarges their capacity to love and serve without limit or exclusion. If the religions do not promote that kind of spirituality, they cannot reflect the One whom we call Creator.

Let us learn from one another. Let us celebrate our shared humanity and collaborate in making this world a better place for all. Let us celebrate our life journeys in all the stages of our lives and make our living a joyful hymn of praise. It is the mystics of all our religions who show us how to move beyond our particularity, without sacrificing it, to come to a genuine sense of what we all share in common. Ira Progoff called it the Well and the Cathedral within:

> Entering the Cathedral
> Wherever we may be
> The center point within us
> Becomes the well
> That opens inward.
> We move into that well
> And beyond it
> Into the buoyant waters
> Of the underground stream
> Where we are now. . .
> Joining those
> Who have been here before us
> In the timeless unity,
> In timeless unity
> Where we are now
> In the silence. . . In the silence. . .[1]

These are symbols of our common spiritual nature, and our powers for regeneration, renewal and rebirth.

No matter what your spiritual tradition, may this book help to affirm, purify, and multiply your mid-life experiences and the great soul making going on in you in the precious days of mid-life and beyond.

We owe a debt of gratitude to the late Betty Lundsted, publisher of Nicolas-Hays, for her interest and encouragement in our work and writings and her care in the revision of *Mid-Life Spirituality and Jungian Archetypes* published in 1999. We are deeply grateful to the Nicolas-Hays' editor, Valerie Cooper for accepting this seminal and now classic book for republication and her care in its revision. Thanks must surely be expressed to Aryeh Maidenbaum, Ph. D, founder and director of The New York Center for Jungian Studies. Dr. Maidenbaum has a commitment not only to Jungian study but to mid-life and beyond. We are proud to have both *Mid-Life Spirituality and Jungian Archetypes* and *Mid-Life Psychological and Spiritual Perspectives* as a part of his Jung on the Hudson series in collaboration with Nicolas-Hays.

## A WORD FROM THE COVER ARTIST, DELLE S. MORRIS

The picture is constellated by the colors in the four fish. In the darkness of the unconscious ideas come through to you from within yourself. Darkness leads to light. The psyche is underground in us all. The underground movement of water is in all of us. We've all gone underwater and recognize how it is. The little fish doesn't know where it is going. It floats up into new territory, propelled by instinct. The little fish shows how instructive these things are. Knowledge comes up through you instinctively, leading you on the path of wholeness throughout mid-life. Ideas are like fish: they can swim through. They suddenly pop up somewhere. You can't control them. Fish illustrate the underquality of thought.

## Notes

1. Ira Progoff, *The Well and the Cathedral* (New York: Dialogue House), p. 147.

# 1

# The Life Cycle

## Psychological Perspectives

Sunrise, sunset, sunrise, sunset
Swiftly flow the days;
Seedlings turn the overnight to sunflow'rs
Blossoming even as we gaze.

Sunrise, sunset, sunrise, sunset
Swiftly fly the years;
One season following another,
Laden with happiness and tears.[1]

The words of Tevye in "Sunrise, Sunset" evoke the movement and the particularity of each stage of the life cycle with its unique joys and sorrows. Tevye has come to understand the life cycle through life experiences and interpretative reflection. The first four lines of the chorus reflect the period of childhood and adolescence; the next four hint at the seasons that are yet to follow. It appears that Tevye has drunk fully of the joys and sorrows of each season. He has a commonsense, experiential knowledge of the life cycle.

Today we live in the era of the scientific study of that commonsense experience. "The true spiritual father of the life cycle theory and of modern adult developmental psychology is Carl Gustav Jung."[2] Daniel Levinson also credits Jung with this.[3] Jung described the life cycle as life in two phases, the first and second halves of life. He saw the primary distinction between the two to be a difference in orientation. The first half of life is lived in two stages, childhood and youth. It is oriented primarily to adaptation and conformity to the outer world. The second half of life, with its stages of mid-life and old age, is oriented primarily to adaptation to the inner world. Jung emphasized that the afternoon of life is not just a pitiful ap-

1

pendage to life's morning but has a significance of its own.[4]

Jung termed the development of the person during the first half of life "ego development." He saw the ego as only a part of the personality, and a subordinate part at that. The ego is the conscious personality. In Jung's psychology, the whole personality, or the Self, is made up of both conscious and unconscious elements. Just as he saw the first half of life as the time for development of the ego, he saw the second half of life as the time for the development of the full Self. This brings to consciousness more and more of the unconscious and reconciles it with the ego. This process is called individuation, which includes integration.

Jung hypothesized that our unconscious is comprised of our personal unconscious and the collective unconscious. What is this mysterious unconscious? We could think of it as the potentialities for awareness or action that the individual has not actualized. These potentialities are the source of ongoing creativity. Creativity is needed at all transition moments, particularly at the transition between the first and second halves of life. We will later discuss the factors in Jung's personality theory in detail. For now, the point is that in the first half of life, through adaptation to our outer environment, we are compelled, all in our own unique fashion, to develop certain aspects of our personalities. No two people have the same ego development.

The human infant needs more constant care and is more vulnerable to abandonment for a longer period of time than the newborn of any other species. We pay our debt to society for this nurturing by developing egos that conform to a large degree with the demands and desires of the people and institutions that surround us. We can hope that some of those people (parents, teachers, etc.) realize that each of us is a unique individual with a unique nature and calling. If this is so, our ego development may genuinely reflect the self. This ego development is found in our response to the personal questions or tasks during the first half of life. What do I like? What people do I enjoy? What work is mine? Answering such questions as these, we come to our identity, primary relationships, and career. Here is the ego, the part of the Self that others see and that the individual knows.

Jung imaged the transition between childhood and youth as a second birth. Until that transition, the child is not able to totally distinguish the ego from the parent. For this reason Jung calls the movement into the second stage of life "psychic birth." We take the step into "psychic birth" laden with presuppositions, and many of them are false. Explaining these presuppositions, Jung wrote, "They may not fit the conditions into which one is thrown. It is often a question of exaggerated expectations, of underestimation of difficulties, of unjustified optimism or of a negative attitude. One could compile a list of the false presuppositions which give rise to the earliest problems."[5]

At first the ego handles these problems and in doing so becomes even stronger. All the while, whole aspects of Self are being denied (contrary aspects of Self are unacknowledged until the second half of life, or the third birth).

If the first half of life is for the development of the ego, the second half of life is for the full flowering of the personality. There is a demand to recenter our lives around a new set of values. To do so, energies we formerly used for external adaptation must be redirected to foster inner growth. The redirection of psychic energy is the essential task of the mid-life transition, according to Jung, and if successfully achieved, creates a renaissance for the mid-life person.

Nature helps. We find a lethargy coming upon us, often for no apparent reason. We find ourselves bored, no longer enthusiastic about the same things. These are inner proddings to let go, to search out new meaning. As Jung wrote, "We see that in this phase of life — between thirty-five and forty — a significant change in the human psyche is in preparation."[6] Still, not everyone will make the transition to the second half of life. We are called, Jung said, to dethrone the idolized values of our conscious world.[7] He saw the moment as a genuine spiritual crisis. This is a difficult task — some think they will lose themselves and hold on in fear. The truth is that they thereby deny the possibility of ever truly finding or becoming their own true selves. Jung believed growth in consciousness to be the key to the movement from stage to stage, the movement to the full flowering of the personality.

Dr. Jung treated many old people. He himself lived and remained active until his death at age eighty-six. If older people had not made the mid-life transition, and if they therefore were living the second half of life by the same principles as the first, they were doomed, Jung believed, to be "hypochondriacs, niggards, doctrinaires, applauders of the past or eternal adolescents — all lamentable substitutes for the illumination of the self . . ."[8]

Old people in the second half of life are like the sun. "After having lavished its light upon the world, the sun withdraws its rays, in order to illumine itself."[9] This is the time to reap the benefits of the inward direction we set out for in mid-life. No longer concerned with adaptation to society, the older person pursues an inwardness that fosters integrity outside and inside the person. Jung thought it right and just that the older person spend time reflectively. When asked in an interview, "What advice would you give older people faced with approaching death?" Jung remarked, "Live on — live on as if you had a hundred years."[10]

In Jung's psychology, belief in an afterlife plays an important role in one's life. Life hereafter is, and has been for centuries, part of our symbolic life. He believed that we must return to and live the symbolic life fully. Not living the symbolic life was, according to Jung, a reflection of the illness of our time.

> It is only possible to live the fullest life while we are in harmony
> with these symbols; wisdom is a return to them. It is neither a
> question of belief nor of knowledge, but of the agreement of our
> thinking with the primordial images of the unconscious.[11]

For Jung, therefore, the old person rightfully looks forward to a new birth in death.

Although Jung's life cycle theory is complex, it also has a simplicity about it. From one stage to another there is a radical break with the past, but the same person or ego still continues. The first birth is, as it were, a drop or expulsion from heaven and the security of the womb, and from that time on, the gradual growth of consciousness takes place with greater momentum. The change that occurs in mid-life far surpasses the adolescent transition in intensity and radicalness and ushers in a time for becoming one's true self. In old age, we reap the benefits of the inwardness developed in the second half of life. Jung perceived that belief in life after death is deeply rooted in the human psyche and urged us to welcome this symbolic myth as part of our human heritage and an important aspect of the fullness of life.

Jung's theories flowed from his own expansion of consciousness and analysis of himself and his innumerable patients. His theories are a construct of the realities he discerned. As the forerunner of the present day life cycle studies, we owe him credit for stimulating the systematic studies that have followed. Some began as early as the thirties, as in the case of Charlotte Buhler. Buhler, a forerunner of humanistic psychology, saw persons developing in a unique way through life. She used the biographical approach in her systematic study. In a desire to understand the person as a whole, the biographical approach allowed her to look at total life histories.

> In looking at life histories of people, we described them in terms of four basic tendencies directed toward fulfillment of life. The four tendencies are: need satisfaction, self-limiting adaptation, creative expansion, and upholding of the internal order.[12]

Jung had initially worked with Freud. It was Freud who got us to see that children were not miniature adults. He emphasized childhood stages and children's consequential psychological growth. Freud's theories, however, also popularized the idea that the personality is rather set at adolescence. It was Erik Erikson, a psychoanalyst and a student of Freud, who took Freud's childhood theories and went beyond them. In 1950 Erikson published his "eight stages" as part of his famous book *Childhood and Society*. Speaking of psychoanalysis, Erikson says,

> . . . Psychoanalysis studies psychological evolution through the analysis of the individual. At the same time, it throws light on the fact that the history of humanity is a gigantic metabolism of individual life cycles.[13]

Erikson's work centered around the psychosocial development of the individual. He depicted certain crisis moments arising as a person progresses through life. Each crisis centers around a particular human task to which the person is summoned. The first is a call to trust. The crisis is, will the child respond to trust and overcome mistrust? Will the child trust that life is gracious? Will the child trust that the caring persons will return? Each crisis comprises a stage, and each stage builds upon another. Erikson cautioned against considering these stages as rungs on an achievement ladder. Nevertheless, the eight virtues, which are the fruit of the eight stages, do comprise the basic qualities of integrated human existence for an individual and for a society.

In Erikson's schema, each stage of life has its own unique series of goals, comprising both internal and external struggles. We reach a degree of wholeness for the particular stage we are in only to find a whole new series of awakenings and demands from within and without. We are never finished products. We are always on the way, in process, or we are fixated and stuck. The wholeness of one stage becomes immaturity when the *same person* being invited or summoned to a new level refuses to go on. In his words,

> . . . We do not consider all development a series of crises: we claim only that psychosocial development proceeds by critical steps — "critical" being a characteristic of turning points, of movements of decision between progress and regression, integration and retardation.[14]

Erikson's conceptualization of the psychosocial developments of the ego confirmed the theory that personality development occurs throughout one's entire life. It does not end along the way, especially not in children. Although his theory advanced the premise that childhood is not the only time for personality development and conceptualizing adult stages of growth, Erikson nevertheless took the short period of childhood and described it in terms of five stages: trust vs. mistrust, autonomy vs. doubt, initiative vs. guilt, industry vs. inferiority, and identity vs. role confusion. He then took the longer period of life, which could well be three-fourths of a person's life, and described that in terms of only three stages:

> young adulthood — intimacy vs. isolation, middle age —
> generativity vs. stagnation, old age — integrity vs. despair

Indeed, each of these periods now needed the same descriptive analysis as the five-stage period of childhood.

Erikson's theory is a construct. It is a way of looking at what goes on as a person grows and matures. It demonstrates ongoing growth, and for many of us it has an intuitive rightness; we respond, "Yes, that seems to describe what really happens." Still, we look for further enlightenment about young, middle, and late adulthood. As late as 1966, Bernice Neugarten, a social psychologist at the University of Chicago, addressed the American Psychological Association and said, "We lack a developmental psychology of adulthood in the sense that we have a developmental psychology of children."[15] At that time, several people were engaged in collecting systematic data on adult stages.

One such person was Daniel Levinson, a social psychologist at Yale University, who started his systematic study in 1966. He began with a desire to understand the mid-life period. At 46, Levinson's experience of profound inner change made him intensely interested in the transition into middle life, both in order to better understand himself and to make a contribution to the field of adult development. "There is a growing desire in our society to see adulthood as something more than a long, featureless stretch of years with childhood at one end and senility at the other."[16]

Levinson began his study with detailed, systematic interviews of 35- to 45-year-old men. He soon learned that to understand the mid-life period he needed to know what preceded and followed it. In other words, the whole life cycle had to be studied in order to comprehend the significance of any part of it. "As our research progressed, it became increasingly clear that a developmental approach was needed in the study of adulthood as of childhood."[17] Levinson also wrote, "The most distressing fear in early adulthood is that there is no life after youth."[18]

Levinson presented the results of his research with men in *The Seasons of a Man's Life*. He died before finishing his research on women. His book gives us a conception of the life cycle as a whole and a more detailed picture of early and middle adult development. Levinson's idea of four "eras" of human development—Childhood and Adolescence, Early, Middle, and Late Adulthood—closely resemble Jung's seasons of life. Levinson calls each era a "time of life." The four eras are compared to four acts in a play. His studies show that chronological ages can be given for the onset of each era and that each is preceded by a transition period that can be both long and complex, as long as three to six years. His unique contribution is in the description of the developmental periods. Each era consists of a sequence of three developmental periods that depict the evolving life structure. According to Levinson's research, each man goes through the same sequence in his own unique way.

22 Years—Early Adult Transition
Early Adulthood
1. Entering Adult World     28 years
2. Age 30 Transition     33 years
3. Settling Down     40 years
45 Years—Mid-Life Transition
Middle Adulthood

    1. Entering Middle Adulthood    50 years
    2. Age 50 Transition    55 years
    3. Culmination of Middle
       Adulthood    60 years

Levinson's schema helps us to see the complexity of adult life. Unlike Erikson, Levinson's is not an ego-development construct, yet his eras and developmental periods are still based upon tasks and crises. He describes adult life as a period of continual movement: we settle down only to experience another eruption. He makes a real contribution by including the "later later years" in his schema. Unlike Gail Sheehy, whose famous book *Passages* ended in the period of the fifties, Levinson takes us through to real old age, even if only briefly.

The field of studying the life cycle is still in its infancy. Much has yet to be done. But a good start has been made and we have learned much from it already. There are many other people who have made great contributions to our understanding of particular aspects of the life cycle. As our other topics are discussed, there will be opportunity to mention Roger L. Gould, Bernice L. Neugarten, Elliot Jacques, Gordon Allport, and Abraham Maslow. But for now, what conclusions can we draw from our reflections on the contributions of Jung, Erikson, and Levinson to our conceptualization of the life cycle?

## CONCLUSIONS

1. Our life is a lifelong journey and personality growth continues from birth to death. We are always in process, always in movement; never grown up (meaning completed), but always on the way.

2. There is a common sequential growth pattern for all the stages of life based upon the tasks of each stage and the periods within the stages.

3. Although the path we follow has a sequential growth pattern that we all share, there is a uniqueness about each individual and his or her growth pattern. No two people are exactly alike or respond the same way. The mystery of ongoing creation still remains.

4. We enter into our own continual creation. Our ongoing

growth is seen in the ongoing choices we make. Unlike the acorn with its natural evolution and automatic growth, human growth is made up of personal choices and decisions.

5. From our earliest childhood stages, assertion of the self is the key to our humanity. Erikson calls it initiative vs. guilt. Rollo May, influenced by Paul Tillich, calls it courage to be and to become:

> In human beings courage is necessary to make being and becoming possible. An assertion of the self, a commitment, is essential if the self is to have any reality.[19]

Every new stage calls for a new assertion of the self.

6. Crisis is a creative aspect of the development of the person throughout the life cycle. Crisis refers to the call or awakening to the new task or movement of growth. If the individual responds, he or she moves on.

7. Creative tension and conflict is essential to human growth.

8. Life is meant to be lived fully at each step along the way. Neither youth nor any other stage is to be idolized. All the stages are necessary to make a whole.

9. At every moment we are more than we seem to be. The conscious self never constitutes the complete person.

10. As we go through life we grow in consciousness. We are called to respond to this new consciousness and to increase our awareness.

11. Although each life transition is crucial and unique, the mid-life transition is a turning point that ushers in a new being that has prime significance for the human fulfillment of the person and the lifelong journey.

12. Mid-life and old age are not dead-end streets but the avenues of the flowering of the true personality.

13. In our early lives we have a primary relationship with our outer environment. The social constructs of society that form us can also imprison our created, gifted selves. In later life we develop a changing relationship to the outer world. In early life, the outer environment is the gatekeeper of our potentialities; in later life, we ourselves become the gatekeeper.

## Theological Perspectives

We have examined how psychology can help us to look at a person's
life cycle and find meaning and significance in the development
and the process of growth that occurs during that life span. And
what of theology? Does theology contradict or complement the
developmental psychologies?

It would be good to begin with asking what we mean by theology.
There is a plurality of theologies. Perhaps some are compatible to
our developmental psychologies and others are not. There was a time
when the theory of evolution was incompatible with our theology.
Today, for most of us it is not. It appears, then, that theology itself
is in change and flux. Could we say it is influenced by its environment, by the people who theologize and their historical, cultural
situation and even their developmental stages? Does theology itself
go through conversions? Can it be retarded, repressed, determined,
neurotic?

For Pope John XXIII, theology had something to do with
renewal, aggiornamento, or "bringing things up to date." Bernard
Lonergan suggests that the obvious conclusion to draw from the
fact that it must have been behind the times, is that it was in need
of being renewed or made new.[20] What is this theology that can be
in need of renewal and can be renewed?

"Theology is a reflection on religion. It mediates between a
religion and a culture. Its function is to bring to light the significance and value of a religion in any given culture."[21] Realizing
that the culture changes and that we ourselves enter into its
re-creation, even as it enters into re-creating us, we sense that
the mediation between culture and religion is an ongoing task
of theology. Theology must, then, always be in the process of
becoming; it can do its job of mediating well or not so well.

But religion itself can be inauthentic and alienating. That is,
rather than express faith in life itself as a gift to me from God, religion can alienate me from my own life, from God, and from genuine
faith. We can at times legitimately speak of religion as pathologi-
cal. Gregory Baum says, "It is possible to read the Scriptures as a
textbook on the pathology of religion."[22] With this in mind, Baum
calls for a "critical theology."

Critical theology is the critical application of the various theories of alienation to the self-understanding in faith of the Christian Churches. This critical method may lead theologians to discover elements of false consciousness in their perception of reality and thus produce a significant change of mind and heart.[23]

Bernard Lonergan also speaks of this change of mind and heart regarding theology.

> Just as reflection on the operation of the scientist brings to light the real foundation of science, so too reflection on the ongoing process of conversion may bring to light the real foundation of a renewed theology.[24]

Abraham H. Maslow in his critique of organized religions suggests that they can and often are the enemies of genuine religious experience. "Conventional religions may even be used as defenses against and resistances to the shaking experiences of transcendence."[25] The thesis of his book *Religion, Values, and Peak-Experiences* is that "organized Religion, the churches, finally may become the major enemies of the religious experiences and the religious experiencer."[26] Religion, he suggests, can be the cause of creating a dichotomy of the transcendent and the secular or profane. In this setup, holy or transcendent events are the domain of the religious and life experiences are simply secular. This is in contradiction to the basic biblical teaching that life itself is holy and that God reveals to us in our life situations. Maslow reminds us:

> When we are well and healthy and adequately fulfilling the concept of "human being," then experiences of transcendence should in principle be commonplace.[27]

Genuine religion sees all of life as sacred. God infused, breathed into us, the gift of life. From the very beginning, humanity has been filled with sacred life. We cannot force the life of a person into compartments, dichotomies, or hierarchies. Each person has one life to live and it is the life of God that connects the self to all of creation. Life is experienced in relationship to all of creation and God, the author of creation. The transcendent experience is the ingredient that has made us human since our creation. Transcendence is first experienced in the ultimate religious questions that erupt out of our very nature. The responsibility of the religions of the churches is to keep the religious questions and all transcendent experiences alive and to maintain the holiness of the true meaning of human existence.

Carl Jung related his dream in which God dropped divine excrement on the Church, shattering it to pieces because it was no longer a source of numinous experience. John XXIII was not quite as dramatic when he demanded that the windows of the Church be opened and the fresh air be let in. Perhaps he also had a dream! Carl Jung, Abraham Maslow, Bernard Lonergan, Gregory Baum, John XXIII—all were intensely committed to human life, to our journey in life, to the transcendent reality in life, to God-called-for renewal, and conversion of theology, religion, and the churches.

We shall proceed by taking the conclusions drawn from our brief encounter with Jung, Erikson, and Levinson and seeing if and how renewed theology is compatible with the life cycle theory.

The understanding of our life experience remains for us the most profound human need. Among our many human experiences are those of great depth that are characterized by being memorable and the source of many decisions. They help to integrate us and our human lives.[28] Baum calls them religious depth experiences. "People become Christians and stay Christians if the Gospel of Christ explains, purifies, and multiplies their depth experiences."[29] Theology in this context is truly pastoral and must deal with the real human lives of people. The Gospel, or any other sacred message, must be the key to understanding our ordinary human life—our life cycle.

> When conversion is viewed as an ongoing process, at once personal, communal, and historical, it coincides with living religion. For religion is conversion in its preparation, in its occurrence, in its development, in its incompleteness, its failures, its breakdowns, its disintegrations.
>
> Now theology, and especially the empirical theology of today, is reflection on religion. It follows that theology will be reflection on conversion. But conversion is fundamental to religion. It follows that reflection on conversion can supply theology with its foundation and, indeed, with a foundation that is concrete, dynamic, personal, communal, and historical.[30]

Renewed biblical theology has restored to us the dynamism of life itself and the journey of faith. Both the Hebrew and the Christian scriptures reflect process. Ongoing conversion is the heart and core of both Testaments. The idea that our personality is being formed throughout life and that at no moment in our life cycle can we say that we are completed or that we have arrived at maturity is in agreement with our theological stance. Although we in faith see our life as a gift from God and understand God as creator, we sense that creation is ongoing in time and history and that we have the freedom to enter into our own ongoing creation in the choices and decisions we make. Part of our humanity is that we are a problem to ourselves and we can reflect upon our problems. At each stage in life we repeat the same questions with greater depth and intensity.

> What am I here for? What is at stake in my existence? . . . No solution is established once and for all. We must all ponder the same question and wonder at the same puzzle again and again.

> Just as I had to go through childhood, adolescence, and maturity, so must I go through the crisis, embarrassments, heartaches, and wrestlings with this basic issue.[31]

William J. Bouwsma believed that in distinguishing between historical and normative Christianity we can find in normative Christianity "a characteristic conception of healthy human maturity."[32] Bouwsma viewed healthy human maturity as the capacity for growth that can be ours at every stage of life. Christian adulthood, for him, is a process we are always moving toward. There is no absolute qualitative difference between the child, the adolescent, and the adult. The adult carries the child within and like the adolescent, the adult is always "trembling to be born." In this sense, normative Christianity has been inclined to accept and even to celebrate the mysteries of the total personality and has incorporated stage development theory, which builds one stage on another, not simply replacing successive stages but absorbing and continuing experiences from stage to stage. For the Christian, Bouwsma says,

> Life . . . is conceived as indefinite growth, itself the product of a full engagement with the temporal experience involving the whole personality.[33]

Regarding the common sequential growth pattern for all the stages of life based upon the tasks of each stage, one is reminded of this beautiful passage from the book of Ecclesiastes:

> There is an appointed time for everything, and a time for every af-

fair under the heavens. A time to be born, and a time to die; a
time to plant, and a time to uproot the plant . . .[34]

Just as Bouwsma saw the essential characteristic of Christian
adulthood to be the capacity for growth, he saw "hardness of
heart," which Jesus spoke of, as the worst state of the human person.
"Hardness of heart" is evidenced in cessation of growth, arrested development, and remaining fixed at any point in life.

> Christian immaturity is the refusal to grow, the inability to cope
> with an open and indetermined future (that is, the future itself);
> in effect, the rejection of life as a process.[35]

The common life cycle can be a profound experience of human
solidarity and at the same time a profound experience of individuality. No two people have the same story or history. We live
through the stages of life in our own unique ways and our styles of
living enter into our continual becoming. "No two human beings
are alike. A major mode of being human is uniqueness."[36] Psalm
139 reflects this personalism and uniqueness:

> Truly you have formed my inmost being; you knit me in my
> mother's womb. I give you thanks that I am fearfully, wonderfully
> made; wonderful are your works.[37]

God, as true artist, knows our uniqueness. And we who are made
in God's image and likeness are called to go about our lives in an
artistic way. We are all called to become our own unique selves. We
are called to a creative dance of life. We are our own choreogra-
phers. We cannot fit into molds; by creative responses and decisions
we respond to the life tasks before us in each stage of life. Carl Jung
reminds us,

> Christianity holds at its core a symbol which has for its content the
> individual way of life of a man, the Son of Man, and that it even
> regards this individuation process as the incarnation and revela-
> tion of God himself. Hence the development of the self acquires a
> significance whose full implications have hardly begun to be
> appreciated, because too much attention to eternals blocks the
> way to immediate inner experience. Were not the autonomy of
> the individual the secret longing of many people, this hard pressed
> phenomenon would scarcely be able to survive the collective sup-
> pression either morally or spiritually.[38]

Jung believed that obedience to awareness is the only true or genuine religion. Mass psychology could well try to pour us into a mold but we are all called to respond to our own growth in awareness, our own expanding consciousness, as the Spirit within us calls us forth even as Jesus was called forth. Is not his public life, ministry, and death a result of the obedience to awareness that called him out of a private existence in Nazareth to share with all of us his uniqueness and call us to our own uniqueness? We must live out of our own depth experiences and the depth experiences of all of humanity. Jung wrote that religion "means dependence on and submission to the irrational facts of experience."[39] I am reminded of Bouwsma's normative Christianity, which, unlike historical Christianity, does not present rational man as the mature adult and repress whole other areas of the human personality. Our own unique depth experiences form our history and our personality even as our personality forms our history and our depth experiences. We are miracles of surprise, continually making critical choices.

The baptism of Jesus can be considered the end of the first period of his life and the beginning of a new period of inwardness and self-assertion, which flows from the ongoing revelation that occurred in him from the time of his conception. The Father proclaimed that self-assertion by saying, "You are my beloved Son. On you my favor rests."[40] The next three years of Jesus' life, beginning with his temptation in the desert and ending with the agony in the garden and death on the cross can be seen as a response to the call of self-assertion. He revealed a new image of God, self, brotherhood, enemies, the Kingdom of God, justice, forgiveness. Jesus' death was the direct result of his integrity and his response to ongoing awareness and depth experiences. He called us to share his expanded consciousness and offered us newness and fullness of life. He invited us to grow beyond the conventional and cultural. He became his own unique self and called us to follow him and also become our own unique selves. As Jung wrote:

> And are not Jesus and Paul prototypes of those who, trusting their inner experience, have gone their own individual ways, disregarding public opinion?[41]

We have no greater way to express our uniqueness than in the personal choice of commitment. In this most personal, unique act, we transcend ourselves even as we create ourselves anew and we foreshadow the embrace of eternal Mystery itself.

But whenever a free and lonely act of decision has taken place in
absolute obedience to a higher law, or in a radical affirmation of
love for another person, something eternal has taken place, and
[humanity] is experienced immediately as transcending the indifference of time in its mere temporal duration.[42]

Crisis, tension, and conflict have a necessary, positive role to
play in the life cycle. Discontentment has the power to open us to
Mystery.

All that is creation in [humanity] stems from a seed of endless dis-
content. New insight begins when satisfaction comes to an end, when
all that has been seen, said or done looks like a distortion.[43]

Discontentment causes us to look beyond ourselves, past the ego,
or self we know. Discontentment and disenchantment force us to
open ourselves to other possibilities, to go beyond present structures
and definitions, and to be truly creative.

Jung said that he could not define who or what God is, but
he could discover the pattern of God in every person he worked
with. Jung was working with our kind of people—people who had
temporarily lost meaning and were searching for it. He was working with people who had collapsed and were struggling to rebuild
their lives in a way that more truly reflected their inner longings
and groping values. They were people who were striving to free
themselves from the deterministic events that engulfed them and
caused their collapse. Sometimes to move from stage to stage, from
smaller consciousness to greater consciousness, we are forced to
collapse, and in that experience of darkness and destruction, a new
way of life is conceived. As John Shea writes,

When order crumbles, Mystery rises. When our most prized
assumptions about life are suddenly ripped from us, Mystery
appears as a fury which threatens to engulf us.[44]

Crisis, tension, conflict, and collapse can be the raw material for
creativity. Each new stage or phase of life needs a creative approach
to move beyond the past into a creative new hope filled with the
new task that it encompasses. In the confusion that results from
crisis, we are forced to search within ourselves to find meaning.
Our experience can be explained by a myth we discover or by one
that erupts from us:

> When humankind attempts to deal with the ambiguity and dis-
> tortedness which is so much a part of history, it "comes upon"
> deeper issues and a larger reality. A mythic story which deals with
> our relationship to the Mystery in which we find ourselves becomes
> the necessary context for creative living.[45]

As we move into a new life stage we encounter "deeper issues and
a larger reality."

Jesus himself explained his own human experience in a mythic
way. "I solemnly assure you, no one can enter into God's kingdom
without being begotten of water and Spirit. Flesh begets flesh.
Spirit begets Spirit."[46]

> I solemnly assure you, unless the grain of wheat falls to the earth
> and dies, it remains just a grain of wheat. But if it dies, it pro-
> duces much fruit. The man who lives his life loses it, while the
> man who hates his life in this world preserves it to eternal life.[47]

". . . and I—once I am lifted up from this earth—will draw all
men to myself."[48]

James Fowler has formulated a structural, developmental theory
of faith stages. Describing the sixth faith stage, Fowler introduces
the person who has entered into "universalizing faith." After being
tried in the arena of life, one is called to the arena of full awareness
and full participation by the providence of God.

> It is as though they are selected by the great Blacksmith of history,
> heated in the fires of turmoil and trouble and then hammered
> into useable shape on the hard anvil of conflict and struggle.[49]

Fowler's empirical studies attempt to correlate predictable se-
quences of formally described stages in the life of faith with the
same stages of human development in general. Although still provisional, there appears to be a faith development that corresponds
to personal human development. As with other stage theories, each
of Fowler's stages is built upon the other, incorporates particular
tasks, and creates a crisis when the task is accomplished. This crisis
is filled with potential for creative growth or radical regression.

Fowler writes, "The faith of Jesus developed under the pressure of
actual conflicts he was engaged in. While the basic elements of his
faith remained, they were reconfigured in terms of his life history."[50] There are normative crisis points throughout the life cycle.

Our ability to fully experience crisis and not run away from it or repress it is to accept the gift of life. The crisis or transition phase can be long. Traditional spirituality refers to it as "the dark night of the soul." Creatively waiting for the light and accepting this limbo period is part of the art of living demanded of us.

In the Incarnation, God takes on our human nature. Many of the teachings of Jesus reflect his own meditation on nature and his understanding that our natural life and life in the Spirit are one and the same great adventure.

> The reign of God is like a mustard seed which someone took and sowed in his field. It is the smallest seed of all, yet when full-grown it is the largest of plants. It becomes so big a shrub that the birds of the sky come and build their nest in its branches.[51]

The dynamics of God's life in us is evinced by the dynamics of growth in the human person—psychic forces at work at every stage to create energy. When Jesus said, "I came that they might have life and have it to the full,"[52] he was expressing the liberation of the dynamics of growth and the liberation of the psychic forces that propel us to grow and to become the fully whole and dynamic human being that he himself became. He shares that with us. He lived a fully human life. Jesus Christ does not give us a second, otherworldly life to live. He graces and liberates the one life God has given us to live so that we can live it "to the full." Life in the Spirit involves living our human life "to the full" at each and every stage.

The Bible portrays people living real, genuinely human lives in which they discover God and themselves. By finding themselves, discovering their own identities, relating to others, and living their own complex daily lives, that God is found not outside all of this but within it. Both the Bible and modern science depict the human person in process. It is in this process that God is involved as creator. God actively affects the way we relate to the world in each and every season of our lives. God is the force propelling us on to a new passage. The "seedlings" are to be cherished for who they are as well as for who they are to become. Each season of life has its own particular characteristics, laws, tasks, and wholeness. Fowler says that each stage has its own particular wholeness, grace, and potential integrity.

It was because Jesus had such a sense of identity and mission (ego) that he found himself carrying the cross.[53] It was because he was confronted by and open to Mystery that he experienced the scandal of the cross and gave over his live and mission (ego). "Father, into your hands I commend my spirit."[54] The conscious and unconscious selves always exist in a paradoxical relationship. We know and we do not know the mystery of our Selves.

Fowler's stages of faith development are described as periods of growth in consciousness. We begin with undifferentiated consciousness and slowly and painfully expand in consciousness so that the full complexity of life, with all its polarities and opposites, are such that only by embracing the complexity can we hope to deal with some of the ambiguity of life. Gradually, as we consciously experience the fact that polarities embrace one another, we return to a unity with full differentiation. Responding to increased awareness and consciousness is responding to the reality of the coming Kingdom of God; this is depicted by the archetypal story of the lion and the lamb.

> Then the wolf shall be a guest of the lamb, and the leopard shall lie down with the kid; the calf and the young lion shall browse together; with a little child to guide them. The cow and the bear shall be neighbors, together their young shall rest; the lion shall eat hay like the ox. The baby shall play by the cobra's den, and the child lay his hand on the adder's lair. There shall be no harm or ruin on the holy mountain; for the earth shall be filled with the knowledge of the Lord; as water covers the sea.[55]

Can we not say that John's baptism of Jesus and the temptations of Christ sacramentalize for us this mid-life crisis and transition? Jesus refers to spiritual rebirth often and that is what the mid-life transition is. Jung tells us that every mid-life crisis is a spiritual crisis. We are called to die to the self (ego), the fruit of the first half of life and liberate the new man or woman within us.

> Those who are called upon to enter the kingdom of God may not always recognize what is happening to them. At first the approach of the kingdom may seem like a violent attack from something dark and dreadful; for when the kingdom descends upon us, the first experience is often a darkening of our old state of mind in order that a new consciousness may emerge. Psychologically this is a necessity. Entrance into the kingdom means the destruction of the old personality with its restricted and uncreative attitudes. If the kingdom is to come, this old person must die. The fortress

behind which the ego has been hiding must be torn down, and as these defenses are battered down forcibly by the movement from within, it may seem at first like a violent assault. Whenever this upheaval in personality occurs, it is important that its religious overtones be realized; for if this dynamic inner process is viewed only clinically, its spiritual significance will be lost and the kingdom will not be revealed.[56]

This radical hope in the second half of life liberates within the person the dormant qualities and aspects of the personality that lie buried within. In becoming his or her true self and in moving toward wholeness, the person is involved in the most profound act of worship. In the early days of the Church, Irenaeus taught, "The glory of God is the human person fully alive." The greatest gift we can give God and others is the gift of our genuine selves. The greatest hope for humanity is the fullness of humanity in another.

As the human person experiences the daily and seasonal deaths and resurrections of human life, which contribute to the development of personality, this inbreak of mystery is a foreshadowing of the future and the coming reign of God.

Since every person is known by God by name, and since every person exists outside of time in the presence of the God who is judgment and salvation, every person is a person of eternity, and not just the noble spirits of history. Moreover it becomes clear in Johannine theology that eternity is seen as existing within time, and that therefore eternity comes to be from out of time, and is not just a reward which is given after time and added to it.[57]

Fowler's stage development theory presents the picture of a person growing in nature and grace through all the seasons of life. The stage-six person is open to the transcendent, responding to awareness with integrity, expanding in consciousness so that even the apparently contradictory becomes congruent. The person with "universalizing faith" is the one moving toward full participation in ultimate communion with the myriad aspects of his or her own personality, all people, and God. This communion is not self-conscious and is fully integrated in a daily life of concern for others. Life here is both loved and held loosely. Psychology would call this the process of interiorization, or integration, or individuation, or growing in self-autonomy, or becoming self-actualized. Theology sees it as becoming the person God calls you to become, responding to the call of creativity, becoming one who is a unique image of God. Throughout the life cycle the human person is engaged in both discovering and unfolding the genuine self.

Gordon Allport sees the religious development of the normally mature and productive personality as a process that evolves through three stages: "The avenue of widening interest (the expanding self), the avenue of detachment and insight (self-objectification), and the avenue of integration (self-unification).[58]

All along the way, faith, hope, and love are necessary ingredients for the growing personality and for movement through the cycle. But nowhere is the demand for faith, hope, and love as great as in the "winter of approaching death." Speaking of death Rahner says,

> Perhaps Christian hope speaks many times in the emphatic way of an initiate, of someone who knows his way around better in eternity with God than in the dungeon of the present. But in reality this absolute fulfillment remains a mystery which we have to worship in silence by moving beyond all images into the ineffable.[59]

At each stage we are called to move into the future, to go beyond what we have come to cherish. Here in old age we are called again to move into the future, to give ourselves over to the Mystery present and beyond us. We are called throughout our life cycle to have faith, hope, and love in life itself, to live fully, and yet to surrender life completely — even as Jesus did.

The mystery of human life is always to be cherished even as it is to be understood as fully as possible. Both psychology and theology are open to the Mystery and willing to seek the facts in observation and scientific study; the two fields are engaged in similar but different aspects of the same tasks. If we need a critical theology we also need a critical psychology. Even as we see the human life cycle as developmental, so too must we acknowledge the fact that both theology and psychology are moving toward a never fully realized understanding.

Our whole life is a movement toward ourself, others, and God. In Ira Progoff's meditation, "The Well and the Cathedral," he speaks of this movement:

> The metaphor of the well represents the individuality and uniqueness of our life, but the further we go into it the more completely we transcend the separateness of our ego-existence. It expresses

the profound paradox that the more we move inward into our privacy and individuality, the more we become connected to the wholeness and richness of the universe. At its deeper levels we experience an expansion of consciousness that enables us to feel we are not limited to being only ourselves. We move through the well of the Self into a dimension beyond it, and that is when we come to the underground stream. Here we experience the Unity of Being and are one with it. It is the place of transcendence where, after a long inward journey, self-transformation and renewal begin.[60]

All of the thousands of people who have participated in the mid-life workshop that we have conducted have expressed some concern about the meaning and purpose of their future lives. During one workshop session, a woman in her late forties enthusiastically spelled out who she then was by creating a mandala or collage that became a self-portrait. She went about it with a zeal that made one feel that even as she placed the pictures and words that represented her on the paper, she herself was both discovering and affirming all she had been, all she was, and all she was yet to become. After sitting for a few moments with two other people in a sharing session, she frantically returned to her work space looking for something that had fallen off the mandala. "I must find it," she said. "It is most important to me. Here it is. Look, it says, 'It is not too late.' I almost thought it was, you know. I'm just finding out it is not." The study of the life cycle, in psychological and theological perspectives, has helped to lift or dispel the image of a second half of life that is without nobility, creativity, or purpose.

### Notes

1. Sheldon Harnick, "Sunrise, Sunset," from *Fiddler on the Roof*, music by Jerry Bock (New York: R.C.A., 1964).

2. Wilbur Bradbury, ed., *The Adult Years* (New York: Time-Life Books, 1975), p. 12.

3. Daniel J. Levinson et al., *The Seasons of a Man's Life* (New York: Ballantine Books, 1978), p. 4.

4. C. G. Jung, *Modern Man in Search of a Soul*, trans. W. S. Dell and Carry F. Baynes (New York: Harcourt, Brace and World, 1933), p. 109.

5. *Ibid.*, p. 100.

6. *Ibid.*, p. 104.

7. *Ibid.*, p. 212.

8. *Ibid.*, p. 109.

9. *Ibid.*

10. Jonathan Stedall, producer, B.B.C. Television documentary, "The Story of Carl Gustav Jung," 1971.

11. C. G. Jung, *Modern Man in Search of a Soul*, p. 113.

12. Charlotte Buhler, "Meaningfulness of the Biographical Approach," in *Readings in Adult Psychology: Contemporary Perspectives*, ed. Laurence R. Allman and Dennis T. Jaffe (New York: Harper and Row, 1977), p. 26.

13. Erik H. Erikson, *Childhood and Society*, 2d ed. (New York: W. W. Norton & Co., 1963), p. 16.

14. *Ibid.*, pp. 270-71.

15. Bernice L. Neugarten, "Adult Personality: Toward a Psychology of the Life-Cycle," in *Readings in Adult Psychology: Contemporary Perspectives*, ed. Laurence R. Allman and Dennis T. Jaffee (New York: Harper and Row, 1977), p. 41.

16. Daniel J. Levinson, *The Seasons of a Man's Life*, p. x.

17. *Ibid.*, p. ix.

18. *Ibid.*

19. Rollo May, *The Courage to Create* (New York: Bantam Books, 1975), p. 4.

20. Bernard Lonergan, *Theology of Renewal*, vol. 1 (New York: Herder and Herder, 1968), p. 34.

21. Bernard Lonergan, *Philosophy of God and Theology* (Philadelphia: The Westminster Press, 1973), p. 22.

22. Gregory Baum, *Religion and Alienation* (New York: Paulist Press, 1975), p. 62.

23. *Ibid.*, p. 194.

24. Lonergan, *Theology of Renewal*, p. 46.

25. Abraham H. Maslow, *Religions, Values, and Peak Experiences* (New York: Viking Press, 1970), p. 33.

26. *Ibid.*, p. viii.

27. *Ibid.*, p. 32.

28. Gregory Baum, *Faith and Doctrine* (New York: Paulist Press, 1969), p. 68.

29. *Ibid.*

30. Lonergan, *Theology of Renewal*, p. 46.

31. Abraham J. Heschel, *Who Is Man?* (Stamford, California: Stamford University Press, 1965), p. 31.

32. William J. Bouwsma, "Christian Adulthood," in *Adulthood,* ed. Erik Erikson (New York: W. W. Norton and Company, p. 1978), p. 81.

33. *Ibid,* p. 87.

34. Eccles. 3:1-8.

35. William J. Bouwsma, "Christian Adulthood," p. 87.

36. Heschel, *Who Is Man?,* p. 37.

37. Ps. 139:13-14.

38. C. G. Jung, *The Undiscovered Self,* trans. R. F. C. Hull (New York: Mentor Books, 1958), p. 60.

39. *Ibid.,* p. 29.

40. Luke 3:22.

41. Jung, *The Undiscovered Self,* p. 69.

42. Karl Rahner, *Foundations of Christian Faith,* trans. William V. Dych (New York: The Seabury Press, 1978), p. 439.

43. Heschel, *Who Is Man?,* p. 86.

44. John Shea, *Stories of God* (Chicago: Thomas More Press, 1978), p. 29.

45. *Ibid.,* p. 62.

46. John 3:5-6.

47. John 12: 24-25.

48. John 12:32.

49. James Fowler, "Stage Six and the Kingdom of God," in *Religious Education,* 1980, p. 236.

50. John Shea, *Stories of God,* p. 134.

51. Matt. 13:31-32.

52. John 10:10.

53. John A. Sanford, *The Kingdom Within* (New York: J. B. Lippincott Company, 1970), p. 35.

54. Luke 23:46.

55. Isa. 11:6-9.

56. Sanford, *The Kingdom Within,* p. 66.

57. Rahner, *Foundations of Christian Faith,* p. 441.

58. Gordon W. Allport, *The Individual and His Religion* (New York: Macmillan Company, 1973), p. 61.

59. Rahner, *Foundations of Christian Faith,* p. 434.

60. Ira Progoff, *The Well and the Cathedral* (New York: Dialogue House, 1977), p. 166.

# 2

# Mid-Life Crisis
# in Theological and
# Psychological Perspectives

When I live in a house which I know will fall about my head in the next two weeks, all my vital functions will be impared by this thought; but if on the contrary, I feel myself to be safe, I can dwell there in a normal and comfortable way.[1]

In mid-life crisis we do not feel safe in our house at all. The roof of our experienced self is falling in, the ground is falling out. Here we are suspended in air, frozen in existential *angst* to surpass all former anxieties, unable to locate or identify this new ache. We are in mid-life crisis and its etiology and teleology are, at this moment in the history of human evolution, the center of gigantic interest and study.

Never before in the history of the human race have so many people approached this anxiety-provoking gap in the life cycle. Never before have so many people lived so long—long enough to stand on the edge of this abyss and pass over or through the ferment into a second half of life. In the past only a few human beings lived into their seventies, eighties, or nineties, but now it is predicted that this life span will be average. Ours, then, are the first generations to experience in "significant population sample" a phase whose features can now be broadly fleshed out and tentatively interpreted.

Before Jung mentions the "roof falling in" in his essay on the stages of life, he states that the discovery of death is a psychically healthy goal toward which one can strive "because shrinking away from it is something unhealthy and abnormal which robs the second half of life of its purpose."[2] While Jung will not attribute the origin and end of mid-life crisis to the fear of death, he does describe it as a symbolic death, which is paradoxically a new birth. His analogy for the illumination of the Self, the holistic development of personality that begins in mid-life, is the sun beginning its decline at noon by withdrawing its rays from the outer landscape and turning them inwards. He warns against trying to carry the sunrise psychology of the youthful phase across the threshold and against shrinking back from the graying thoughts of approaching age.

Jung's analysis of this passage, unfolding so much more than the fear of death, is extremely complex but energizing and exciting. We will draw largely on his vision while looking to integrate into it the perspective of many developmental psychologists. We will also probe this existential crisis from the faith vision of Judeo-Christian tradition to see how the life stage and critical theology reflect new life and light upon each other in this encounter. If real theologizing is done by reflecting on conversion,[3] this crisis is the moment that calls for conversions more than any other a person ever experiences. If a critical theology can enlighten the believer regarding the life cycle, it certainly can illuminate this most critical phase of all, the mid-life transition.

Both Levinson and Gould see a symbolic death at this threshold. Gould sees that the major false assumption carried from childhood that is challenged in the mid-life decade is, "There is no evil or death in the world. The sinister has been destroyed."[4] Role reversal with aging parents (which eventually moves toward the death of a parent) is compounded when children are moving out at the same time. As children shut the doors on their "out-of-it" fifty-year-old parents, the terror of death may open its doors. Gould quotes a thirty-seven-year-old executive: "Up to this point life was all uphill with no thought of the end; now it's as if I'm at the crown of the hill and can see the downslope for the first time. Death is a long way off but it is definitely there."[5]

Levinson sees that the end of the omnipotent feeling of youth comes as a message of mortality, destruction, and separation. He cites an anxiety about disease and dying as a real and new part of the horizon of the person as the mid-life transition begins. "Our profound anxiety at passing forty reflects the ancient experience of the species. We still fear that life ends at forty."[6] His studies of those who move through the transition and further into the mid-life period supports Jung in his notion that fear of death becomes remote when the major polarities of young/old have been dealt with. It moves once more to its customary slot in the back of the mind.

For Elliot Jacques, however, the central and overbearing issue at mid-life is coming to terms with one's own mortality. For Erikson it is the Generativity/Stagnation conflict, and for Bernice Neugarten it is growing interiority. Each of these is on to some real aspect of this inner/outer movement. There is an emerging consensus from psychology that the whole mid-life movement is crisis, which should initiate a transition, and finally emerge into a period or stage. The stage is variously called Middle Adulthood, Middle Age, Mid-Life, the Autumn, the Afternoon of Life. It may be a very long period. It is particularly dramatic for the woman who can look forward to at least thirty-five more productive years after her childbearing period is over.

What is the mid-life crisis and how does one make it successfully to the sunlit afternoon? As hard as it would be to say it to someone who is experiencing the feelings of "the roof falling in," or fearing that the foundations of her life are crumbling, or that her youth is slowly dying, the crisis is more than these peripheral symptoms. The crisis is the earth-shattering peril and potential of the mid-point challenge: will we or will we not negotiate the profound changes presaged in the withdrawal of energy from the structure we have built for some forty years—the "I am"—to become more our own true selves? Will we relinquish the false assumption that the truths and ideals of young adulthood will continue to energize us as they have? "We cannot live the afternoon of life according to the programme of life's morning, for what was great in the morning will be little at evening, and what in the morning was true will at evening become a lie."[7]

The significance of the morning was our development as a conscious individual; for Jung, our ego development. This achievement, our basis for decision-making up to now, was the personal myth by which we were living. It spawned the roles we played, the relationships we formed. It was the Dream, the values, the story from which we lived our lives. It was the choice of life-style and commitments, the choice of a ladder to climb, and promises to keep. It was the measure of falls and infidelities. It may have been children we bore or discoveries we made in a lab or a hospital or a kitchen. It may have been the excuse for alcoholism or worka-holism. It was an apartment, a rectory, a loft in the city, or a city itself. It was kudos sought, titles and degrees, money made and lost, charge cards, registration voting cards, religious conversions and affiliations, faith development or agnosticism. It was social services rendered, committees joined, games played and watched. It was a secure masculinity or femininity or gay community, crimes commit-ted or a commitment to drifting.

The forty- or fifty-year-old has barely said, "This is who I am and who I will be," when he may be toppled from this place of arrival and begin all over again to ask, unconsciously at first, and then more and more painfully in myriad ways, "Who am I, really?"

The mid-life crisis is relatively, not strictly, chronological. Like all development crises, it is something that occurs to help one move on to another stage. In this sense, it is not something negative but a positive opportunity. For some people who allow it its full flood, this, the severest crisis of all, with possibly the most earth-shaking feelings, will be the moment of profoundest conversion. However, we are all so different that for some smooth evolvers, the profound questions may be asked and answered calmly; but even then the conversion will be just as profound or the atrophy just as horren-dous. Others may be sucked into unresolved earlier crises. Some will deny, regress, or become petrified until (if ever) their lives are loosened again and they move through this transition.

> The mid-life crisis is a stormy transition period that is marked by
> internal changes, by conflicts and challenges. Like the turbulent
> period of adolescence, it leads to a new and calmer stage of life:
> middle age. But unlike the earlier crisis that which occurs in the
> middle years still seems mysterious and is often misunderstood.[8]

Mysterious indeed! We need to recognize the danger and the promise of this crucial turning point. The real crisis is not the turbulence, the depression, the mid-life "crazies," as important as these outer signs of it may be. The crisis is: Will I move on? Will I leave behind the first half of my life, which then demands a whole new myth and story for me to live out of, a whole new meaning and way of being? Or will I continue with no exit to live out of my lost youth, like Sisyphus, over and over again? Will I follow the legions who may be short-circuiting crisis by finding a sports car and a new young husband or wife and starting the first half of life all over again, different but the same? Will I go on choosing new and different outer-oriented projects, keeping up with the Joneses, robbing myself of all the potential of a second journey and a more clearly immanent *and* transcendent story?

The crisis, then, *is* the transition in its alpha and omega, that transition when we do or do not repattern our lives and begin to rework our personalities. Jung's schema presents four life stages: childhood, youth, mid-life, and old age. The transition between youth and mid-life is far more radical than the earlier or later transitions. In the first two periods, childhood and youth, we are primarily outer-directed. We are socialized, domesticated, pushed and pulled to fit into the outer world. Parents and all surrounding adults direct our lives until we ourselves take over pushing and pulling to fit in. The adolescent who moves out, in a great act of freedom and self-liberation, with all its attendant tearing away and tearing down, becomes the young adult. Jung calls this the second birth. It is the psychic birth when the individual consciousness emerges from the womb of the parents' ideals and non-ideals, morality and amorality, sanity and insanity. However complete or incomplete this break (and who does not continue to perform for parental approval?), young adults are still primarily outer-directed. Although they can choose the rules they will follow, their lives are bound by an essential conformity. Will I marry? There is a statistical average age for marriage that moves up and down in each society, in each generation. Which structure will I give myself to as novice? Corporate, domestic, literary, agricultural, small business, art, theater, church, health care, cottage industry, construction, child nurturing, political, scientific, educational? Each has its game and its rules. Will I be counterculture? Will I follow the drop-out rules, the missionary route, the religious community route? Culture is still what I am countering. In this stage I will still be told what to do verbally and nonverbally, even though I now choose the tellers and can move from group to group and grow into some autonomy.

All my initiatives and energies will be outer-directed, like the sun in the morning when

it rises from the nocturnal sea of unconsciousness and looks upon
the wide bright world that lies before it in an expanse that steadily
widens the higher it climbs in the universe. In this extension of its
field of action caused by its own rising, the sun will discover its
significance, it will see the attainment of the greatest possible
height, and the widest possible dissemination of its blessings as its
goal. In this conviction, the sun pursues its goal to the unforeseen
zenith — unforseen because its career is unique and individual,
and the culminating point could not be calculated in advance. At
the stroke of noon, the descent means the reversal of all the ideals
and values that were cherished in the morning. It is as though it
should draw in its rays instead of emitting them. Light and
warmth decline and are at last extinguished.[9]

Who could look at the self-contained orb of the red setting sun
and not see in its perfect circumference cavernous, burning fire, the
antithesis of the impossible-to-look-at noon munificence? Yet the
setting sun does give light, more magnificent because of its red and
violet withholding, and the morning sun does indeed have its inner
white core.

The 30-year-old is wonderfully cheerful, hard working, obedient
to the demands of daily routines. The imagery of the ladder is
central to this period, which Levinson calls "Settling Down." It
reflects the concern for advancement and affirmation: "By ladder,
we refer to all dimensions of advancement; increases in social rank,
income, power, fame, creativity, quality of family life, social contribution, as these are important for the man and his world."[10]

Levinson studied men. Ascending is no less important to the
thirty-year-old woman, even when her step-by-step ascent has a
different context, style, and priorities. This is a fruitful period for
her, rich in experience. If she is a primary nurturer of marriage,
children, a cause, or a career, she is pouring herself out on them,
and their demands on her are all-consuming. She is moving up-
ward, facing outward, radiating light and warmth. One hopes both
women and men maintain a fidelity to their inner core. In the first
half of life, people who are becoming self-actualized are attempting
to build their empires, however influenced by conformity, however
external, on the rock of their own true selves, not simply on the sand
of other's expectations.

What happens then at the zenith? One man in our mid-life workshop put it this way:

> The spark is gone, or at least fading fast. Somehow there is doubt and somberness threaded into almost everything I see, touch, and do. I fear where I did not use to fear. The old answers don't seem adequate. I'm too old to be afraid, to have doubts, to wonder. I knew I was haunted by perfection. I know it more now. I have to get away from black and white. I have to stop running so quickly to vague places for vague reasons. I need a goal but I'm afraid to choose one—what if I screw it up?

Another woman explained, "I feel restless and flat and concerned about the future. I have a feeling of being adrift; I'm not so sure of all the answers as I was earlier in life."

Where do we go for the answers when this whole passage and stage is so new to the race? We are the pioneers. Where do we find the way? Jung would say that our own answers are within each of us. Jesus spoke of the will of God and the Kingdom together, and said that the Kingdom of God is within. Moonwalks and exploring Saturn and Mars were wondrous feats. Yet the whole thing happened when human beings reached into themselves and imagined that it could be done; reached into their historical, communal experience to imagine how it could be done. Then they began experimenting, made and corrected mistakes, and finally, the launch happened. These were marvelous movements of faith in, hope in, and love for a project. The infinity of these outer journeys and goals magnifies for us the immense possibilities that lie within human consciousness. Even though these are journeys into outer space and largely mechanical feats, calling on a small area of the rational, analytical thinking of human consciousness, they turn our attention dramatically to the infinite possibilities of our inner worlds. For Jung, for the religions of the world, and from our Judeo-Christian view of the human person informed by modern science, each of us has an inner world so vast that we are the consciousness of the universe. As the consciousness of the universe, we contain and transcend the vastness of space with all its heavenly bodies, all of creation, and find the roots of this human spirit in the infinity and eternity of the Creator. The myth of "God up there" in the heavens and we down here no longer works as an image of immanence and transcendence. That is the God who was proclaimed dead in the sixties. Thy myth of the God who is both within and "more than" is very much alive. Living myths create images of truth for us.

It is to the "within" and the "more than" that mid-life crisis beckons. The stirrings of the crisis move us to turn our attention to the voice from that inner world that has been speaking our self from the first moment of conception. As we have grown, we have developed some parts of that self. If our inner processes have been healthy, more and more of our unique possibilities have been noticed and integrated. The forces of the first half of life have called forth certain potentials of our personalities and left others untouched. In relationships, for example, immense parts of self are called forth as we turn each different, unique face to the person who calls it forth. The attitude and functions we use with ease have become highly developed. Jung's typology tells us that each of our conscious psychologies is a more introverted or a more extroverted attitude, and that either intuition or sensing is more developed as a function of perception, while thinking or feeling is more developed as a function of judgment. Consequently, one of the attitudes and functions is primary, and its opposite is inferior, deep in the unconscious, undiscovered self. Jung used the types as a compass for the voyages in the undiscovered self. Knowing from a person's type what could be known of his or her conscious psychology leads to its opposite, the personal nature of the unconscious, and is thus a way to set a person on the road to individuation. Individuation is the task of the second half of life. It means becoming one's own true self. In part, it means integrating our inferior attitiude and functions.

In 1928, Jung wrote:

> But one thing I must confess: I would not for anything dispense with this compass (type theory) on my psychological voyages of discovery . . . I value the type theory for the objective reason that it provides a system of comparison and orientation which makes possible something that has long been lacking, a critical psychology.[11]

The commitments we make, whether to mastery of self or the environment, moral and altruistic concerns, or to self-protection from involvement, will profoundly influence what parts of our personalities are developed in the first half of life. Majorie Fiske, who uses this commitment framework for examining psychosocial change in adulthood, quotes a prosperous forty-five-year-old, who says to a peer with earnestness and a touch of surprise, "I've learned a lot in the past twenty-five years, but unfortunately its all about petroleum."[12]

No matter how little or how much of our personality has been developed, there still is a whole other side of us left undeveloped. If we do not make the transition from outer-directed life designing, then the same aspects of personality characteristic of the first half of life will continue to be called forth in us. Dormant within our psyches, however, our personalities and our spirits are whole areas that were not touched or incarnated in the first half of life. These are only unfolded, called forth, and touched if we make the inner search and move toward the wholeness of individuation, becoming our own true selves. These opening lines from Christopher Fry's drama, *A Sleep of Prisoners*, might well be a description of the mid-life crisis and transition:

> Thank God our time is now when wrong
> Comes up to meet us everywhere.
> Never to leave us till we take
> The longest stride of soul man ever took
> Affairs are now soul size
> The enterprise
> Is exploration into God.

This inner search through soul-sized affairs, this enterprise of exploration into God will take each of us in crisis, during transition and beyond, through our whole self, as Jung saw it, conscious and unconscious. We will need to personally discover the deepest ultimate meaning about ourselves, the one that has so vibrated in millions through the generations that it has been doctrinalized. We will need to penetrate the Mystery that we are created and incarnate sons and daughters of God. We will need to look in prayerful awe at this self, and this cosmos, and this God which each of us reflects and incarnates. We will need to explore the story we have lived out of, the story our lives have told and is telling. We will need to look at the values each of us embodies in choices. Finally, we will need to create our future over and over again, as we imagine, make and correct mistakes, launch out, and live until death and beyond.

We will look at all this later. For now, we will go through the door to the inner self, which opens in the midst of the crumbling meaning of mid-life crisis. For as John Shea says:

> Our relatedness to Mystery generates a quest for meaning which functions in an ultimate way. . . . It is at the limits of human powers that the quest for meaning becomes most acute. When we cannot explain the events which engulf us, when we cannot endure the suffering which overwhelms us, when we cannot bear the evil which defeats us, we do not become submissive but highly imaginative. We formulate symbols which account for and even celebrate the darkness and ambiguity. . . . The instinct to meaning will not be denied.[13]

Research into consciousness that has occurred during this century has shattered the former limited conceptions of the human mind. The unconscious (and in Jung's theory, the collective unconscious) remain areas of tremendous mystery. Engaging this mystery of the eruption of our unexplored self will give new meaning.

> For nausea and anxiety do not result from too many dead ends and futile elements in our lives. They really come about because there is too little mystery in our lives.[14]

If a friendly attitude can be established toward these messengers from our unconscious, they will speak in images, metaphors, and symbols. Christian spirituality has always maintained a strong sense of the human mind with its unfathomable depths since it knows that humanity shares in the mysteriousness of the Unfathomable One as image and offspring. Religion and spirituality have always spoken the language of myth, symbol, metaphor, and ritual. Modern psychotherapy has rediscovered the importance of this illumination by metaphor through an openness to the myth and symbol of our experience, waking and sleeping.

What are the metaphors, myths, and symbols of the crisis? What are the images which our "strung-out" emotional lives are trying to envision? What are the metaphoric messages from the inner self? Ultimately, each person must answer this question for himself or herself. It can be helpful to find the images that lie behind our own crisis emotions. If we allow ourselves to have a bodily sense of our feelings and wait for an image to come to us, the feelings may shift.[15] We may eventually penetrate the images to understand their meaning, from which we may find our own unique answers. Some of this has been done indirectly by the developmentalists who have broadly and generally interpreted the feelings of people in the mid-life crisis. Their work may help us to name and differentiate our *own* feelings and our *own* new truths for the afternoon of life. When these can be further illumined by the transpersonal truths—the myths and symbols of the Judeo-Christian tradition—each of us can be further grounded in meanings that put us in touch with the transcendent dimension in and beyond us. This may lead to more willing detachment from outer-directedness.

A myth (as we use the term here) does not speak primarily of events of the outside world but of themes of the inner world of the imagination. Their archetypal, essential forms are the same all over the world even though the narratives draw their structures from different environments and cultures. Jung interprets them as archetypes of the collective unconscious. From the beginning, the myths of Christianity effected great spiritual growth because they expressed so completely the mystery within the heart of humanity and the elements of every human story. Because of this, there is a special transpersonal magnetism and power generated when a person's story at a crucial turning point makes contact with a Christian myth that can penetrate it.

Lethargy, apathy, monotony, indifference, impotence, frigidity, uncertainty, listlessness, dawdling over tasks, loss of interest in things that were once of vital concern; going through the motions, boredom—these are familiar constellations of crisis feelings. An image that may rise from these is "suspension in mid-air." Jung uses this phrase to describe his disorientation in what Gould[16] interprets as the beginning of Jung's period of mid-life crisis when, at 37, he broke from Freud. What does such a state of suspension tell us? Perhaps, to use another Jungian image, that psychic energy has been withdrawn from the conscious ego and given over to the unconscious. It may be telling us that what formerly got us up and out every morning no longer has the same power to compel us. It is a message that this is a time for different enthusiasms, if we can bring ourselves to believe that enthusiasm will ever be possible again. As one person described her image, "I felt like my life had been canceled. Like I'm closed for repairs, only I may be unable to be repaired."

Is all this dullness perhaps the graphic premonition of the Generativity/Stagnation polarity with which Erikson characterizes the whole mid-life period or the young/old polarity Levinson uses? This "suspension in air" is a stagnation and sense of oldness that feels terrible. It is a kind of deadness and burial. Is it not a solitude? A dark night of the soul? This is a frightening experience when the person has in the past experienced only short periods of boredom. Now one's sense of time completely breaks down. This lethargy is really a loss of both past and future. The uselessness of the past meshes with an inability to move on. Barbara Fried reminds us that in medieval days this was called *Acedia,* and it was a deadly sin.[17] It was a deadly sin because it was thought that one who experienced such deadness of heart had lost the sense of place in the divine scheme of things and had thus lost the sense of the mercy of God.

The order of Christendom, with its hierarchies reflecting the order of the stars and planets, eventually broke down and Acedia became lost to us as a deadly sin. Yet, as our renewed contact with a Christian mythology removed from the outer spheres of geography, astronomy, and social order rises again from within the collective unconscious in a dynamic world view, Acedia returns, not as a deadly sin but as an angel of light, warning us of the great choices ahead. The choice will be to change or die. These feelings are indeed a loss of faith, hope, and love in the past and future. They are a loss of contact with our ongoing story. This is a clue to our cure. It may come from a recovery of that story. Apathy may begin to subside as suddenly as it came on us as we engage in the process of making peace with our past, through recalling, objectifying, and owning as much of our story as possible.

Memory, when it occurs in the infant, is one of the first signs of budding consciousness. As such it is the doorway to the "I am." Our sense of time and the ongoing narrative sense that underlies all our thoughts are connected to it. Memory, time, story, identity are connected as are all hints of transcendence, the kingdom of God within. Research has revealed that cancer occurs when DNA "forgets" the code that allows the individual cell to perform in harmony with the whole body. This other "forgetting" of the past, present, and future by losing hold of their meaningfulness, this moment when "our house" begins to fall down around us, is filled with the foreboding of dying and annihilation. "Man understands his present only insofar as he understands it as the approach toward and the opening of the future."[18]

If we allow ourselves to experience these feelings and not to regress to a round of activity, allow them to really speak their image or word to us, and then touch and awaken within once more or for the first time the most fundamental of all Judeo-Christian myths, the creation myth, the essential generativity story, we may move or be moved into the third birth. This will be the birth of the true Self, which may then, through the second half of life, be structured in life-styles that truly reflect this self.

We bring a new consciousness from the space age to the poetry of Genesis. We bring a new consciousness from our own middle age to that poetry. When in our own stagnation we read that the world was created from nothingness and chaos, we can truly identify. We can read it anew, now that somehow all this infinite space and time and all the energy and matter they have generated are seen to be *within* consciousness. First of all, it is within each of us because we are the product and knowing spirit of the whole cosmos. We are chemical descendants of stars. We are the meaning-makers of the whole thing. Our explorations of scientific truth have revealed this wonder to us. It and we are within in another, more significant sense. This we know from the other kind of truth, mythic truth, proclaimed in the revelation of Genesis. We are each within the knowledge, the beneficence of the one who said: "Let there be . . ."[19] and "It is very Good."[20] Man and woman, each of us, is Image, "spitting image," reflection, mirror, epiphany of a tremendous lover. Each of us is envisioned, known through and through. As Jesus said, "The very hairs of your head have been counted."[21] To be created, Jesus told us, is to be the child of the generativity of a father, and therefore, to see any of us, as to see Jesus, our brother,[22] is to see the Father.[23]

To be within in this way is to be intimate. It is to be loved in an intimate, infinite way. When such a love penetrates our shell of alienation and apathy (and this can happen in the dark[24] and in the solitude of crisis when nothing is quite enough), a person can fall in love in an unrestricted way. Such a falling in love is what Bernard

Lonergan calls a religious conversion.[25] It is a whole change of horizon—in this case, ultimate horizon. Since such changes of horizon
can occur at each passage, religious conversions are possible at each
such juncture. Are there not perhaps built-in grace moments as well
as the Spirit's surprises?

> Now, I believe that the mystical life ordinarily develops through
> these Jungian stages of death and rebirth because in mysticism,
> as I have frequently stated, one does not transcend the human
> condition but becomes authentically human under the guidance
> of faith and love.[26]

The emphatic statement of Genesis is not merely that the whole
of creation is the image of the Creator, though that is certainly
implied, but that each woman, each man, is an image.[27] As we
hover at the top of the ladder, bored by climbing, apathetic about
taking another step, we desperately need to be caught up in the
vision, belief, and promise that each of us, when we are true to
ourselves, is a unique, individual, irreplaceable reflection of God.
God tells my story. I tell God's story. I need to know that everything
is within, because within me and within the cosmos, *I* open out to
God. Because this is my source and my reason for being, I can never
be wiped out or annihilated, all appearances to the contrary.[28] I have
and will always have infinite significance. Every breath I take has
meaning. The life I live through and beyond my body, even now as
I interpret and interpenetrate reality outside physical contact, will
never end.

> We do not project something from the future into the present, but
> rather in man's experience of himself and of God in grace and in
> Christ, we project our Christian present into the future.[29]

Even more important good news at this midpoint juncture is that
if this is so, then my potential is all there already. Everything I need
is really at my fingertips. The whole repatterning that I have to do
in the future, in the second half of life, can come from within the
Self. This inner architectural projection just awaits the materials I
will choose from the local scene.

I can get in touch with my past to forgive it and to build on its
strengths because, like the future, it is all there within me and
within the mind of the all-forgiving, all-transforming God. I just

have to open myself to that forgiveness and transformation. The myth has such power because it says that Christ, the "image of the Invisible God," is "the first born of all creatures who has achieved reconciliation for each of us so that we might be free of reproach and blame."[30] It is powerful because it also says that God goes before us in cloud by day, in fire by night. God goes before us in our very own potential, so we have nothing to fear. "Despite this you would not trust the Lord your God who journeys before you to find you a resting place."[31]

Regret, anger, self-doubt, doubt about all relationships and commitments, religious doubt, anxiety, threat; feeling imprisoned, trapped, desperate, hopeless, tortured, hemmed in, restless, dissatisfied, morose, melancholy, nauseated, despairing, fearful: these all form another characteristic gestalt of crisis feelings. These kinds of feeling are a more active torment than the numbness of the other set. They are perhaps the signs of the terrible conflict within the self. This emerges as the desire and temptation to tear down in frenzied anger all that one has built. The successful person is confronted with the aching "So what?", the unsuccessful with "I'll never make it now!" There is a desire to take revenge on the foolish ego, which has wasted so much time and squandered so much precious and now limited energy on so many useless projects. The images and symbols that rise out of this kind of conflict are perhaps those of self-loathing and eternal damnation. "This kind of negative experience tends to reverse one's love-hate relationships. If a person formerly idolizes his life, he is now inclined to demonize himself."[32]

Are not these premonitions of Erikson's last polarity, the Integrity/Despair conflict, and the Immortality/Mortality polarity of Levinson? There is a terrible danger of getting stuck here and withering up and becoming bitter and Scroogelike, continuing acquisitiveness for want of anything new to do. The self-hatred of the despair can encircle and encompass everyone and everything else.

One who would not despair must engage all these feelings and deabsolutize them. "At every crisis one meets the unknown, one relates to it by struggling with it, by wrestling with it."[33] I have doubts and regrets and anger, but I am more than my doubts and regrets and anger. I am not determined or imprisoned by my past. I am also my present and my future, and I can change. I am not trapped by my commitments, I can rework them. "The negative crisis feelings can make a person aware of what his real call is *not*. In this disclosure of what his real call *is not*, there appears a first glimpse of what it might be."[34]

Besides allowing one's self to feel these feelings without repressing or drugging them, faith and hope in the present can come again from remembering the past and its conflicts, and the survival, and sometimes growth, that arose from them. Learning to form an image of the future is a source of hope in despair. Storytelling, meditation, and prayer can be important to these processes, as is bringing one's values to consciousness.

> Faith, just as love, demands that we embrace our human history and vibrate to its inner possibilities both now and prospectively, not trying to sidestep or bracket it. If our faith leads us to disdain the human situation and seek the Lord apart from it, this is more a subtle form of despair than faith. Jesus the Word who became incarnate in our history awaits us at the end of and through our human future, not apart from it.[35]

Such a loosening of the soil of one's life may result in intellectual and moral conversion. Lonergan includes intellect, morality, and religion as distinct dimensions of conversion.[36]

Jung points out that the heavier crises of faith, often resulting in psychological illness, occur after the age of 35. As a result, his life-long primary concern was with the failure of meaning in adult lives. This must be a primary concern of religion and theology. A failure of meaning, such as the one heralded by this constellation of negative feelings, certainly calls for a conversion. Perhaps the horizon that most needs to be ministered and received is the one lit by the myth of Incarnation. At this point, one needs a reappropriation of one's humanity, a second naïveté to displace the loss of naïveté and innocence.[37]

The Incarnation myth says to all who want to be "god" that God became human. There is a phantom of perfection that haunts the hallways of the human psyche. People live their lives either running toward it or away from it. Each human being seems to have a fantasy of someday having it "all together" and seems to live life and climb ladders in the shadow of this idealized godlike self. This is a distortion because it absolutizes the *imago dei* of the Creation Myth.

This urge pushes people from book to book, relationship to relationship, group to group, expert to expert, crime to crime, movement to movement, cause to cause, life-style to life-style, bed to bed, looking for the advice, the answer, the key that will once and for all ensure perfect happiness and fulfillment, fill emptiness, and still restlessness. It is a trigger for anger and depression when each time something or someone proves to be less than the "key." At the midpoint between the morning and afternoon of life, one touches the apex of this disappointment, now noticing not only the inadequacy of everything one has tried but one's own decaying inadequacy and real un-godlikeness.

The Incarnation myth tells of solidarity, oneness with never finished, imperfect humanity; God at one with the human condition. In Jesus Christ, Christian faith sees God living humanly. The core mystery of Christianity is God living humanly within the boundaries of a little, conquered, Middle Eastern country, within all the limitations of being human, in pain, in a wearing-down human body, in the midst of injustice and in conflict with others who would not accept his being himself, saying what he said, and doing what he did. The Incarnation is not a denial or rejection of this petty world or this weak humanity but an assimilation of it.

Incarnation means enfleshment, not merely playing at being human and hiding behind a make-believe body, but being one of us and with us. This is Christianity's core teaching about God. The significance of this is that we find our godliness precisely in our humanity. Jesus' life is a blinding manifestation of the presence of God in all creation. He inherited genes, breathed this atmosphere, and learned a language, culture, and trade which connected him to the whole of history. He is never what we image godliness to be, an aloof, esoteric figure removed from or preaching hatred of this grimy, imperfect, material existence. He shocks us by his disregard for even the accepted distinction of clean and unclean. He is not impermeable. He does not use people or things. The individual human person was always the supreme value for him. He shared the life blood of his Jewish brothers and sisters and took their burdens upon himself. He felt frustrated and angry, and wept because they wouldn't believe him. He suffered humiliation from their false accusations and mockery. He was exhausted from unceasing demands for healing. He really got involved with people. He felt the pain of their blindness, leprosy, loss. He identified with the con-

demnation and ridicule heaped on public sinners. He agonized over
the hardheartedness of the Pharisees and leaders. How many times
before the cross must he have said, "Father, forgive them; they
don't know"![38]

Hoping in the midst of human suffering and living, he transformed the pain he experienced into physical and emotional healing for some, regeneration and transformation for others. Precisely
through solidarity with the human condition and trust in individuals, he communicated faith, hope, and love, and people grew
and were healed in his presence. He suffered being human from
birth to death, but he did not preach mere acceptance of pain and
evil. He was not simplistic. He preached transformation of pain and
evil and lived by this precept. He warred against sickness, suffering,
and death. He preached love, even of those who caused his suffering, inflicted his pain and planned his death. He patiently with-
stood the suffering that came from others, while he warred against
the physical, emotional, and moral sufferings that tear people apart
from within.

Incarnation means that he had to suffer all these things "so as to
enter into his glory."[39] Entering into his glory was his recognition as
Lord and God.

> What was necessary was that the likeness should be seen through
> to the end in every respect, so that he might become merciful and
> faithful as their high priest before God.   (Hebrews 2:17)[40]

Jesus handled the facts and the struggles and imperfections of his
living; he did not omnipotently avoid his human struggles. This
reveals him as *the* image of God. His refusal to come down from the
cross evinces an unwavering fidelity to his postconventional consciousness; he died trusting in his intimacy with the Father, reveal-
ing the Resurrection through which he lives on in his Spirit in all of
humanity and creation.

We need to pierce once for all in the Spirit of Christ the bubble of
perfection and the divinizing and absolutizing of any outer reality.
We need to find the beauty in our own "missing pieces" that keep us
searching and striving to fill the hole deep within us. Just as we need
to accept the marvel of our being an image of God, we need to love
ourselves as *only* an image and an imperfect one. This is both the
marvel and the lure of being human. We need to always be in process. We need to suffer all these things so as to enter our glory. At the

zenith of youth we feel a hatred of that youth, and a worse hatred of coming age. If we drink this cup to the bottom we find with the God-Man of our race that the wheat and weeds grow up together; that hate can be transformed into love; that real resurrection comes through real death. Then as our "outer house" crumbles, we will feel completely safe as we begin to rebuild the new outer structure from the core of our own individual identity.

## Notes

1. Carl G. Jung, "Stages of Life" in *The Structure and Dynamics of the Psyche, Collected Works of C. G. Jung*, vol. 8, trans. R. F. C. Hull (Princeton: Princeton University Press, 1960), para. 791.

2. *Ibid.*, para. 791.

3. Bernard Lonergan, "Theology in Its New Context," in *Theology of Renewal* (New York: Herder and Herder, 1972), p. 243.

4. Roger L. Gould, *Transformations: Growth and Change in Adult Life* (New York: Simon and Schuster, 1978), p. 217.

5. *Ibid.*, p. 229.

6. Daniel J. Levinson, *The Seasons of a Man's Life* (New York: Ballantine Books, 1978), p. 330.

7. Jung, "Stages of Life," para. 783.

8. Nancy Mayer, *The Male Mid-Life Crisis* (Garden City: Doubleday, 1978), p. 248.

9. Jung, "Stages of Life," para. 777.

10. Levinson, *The Seasons of a Man's Life*, p. 59.

11. Carl G. Jung, "A Theory of Types," in *Modern Man in Search of a Soul*, trans. W. S. Dele and Cary Baynes (New York: Harcourt, Brace and World, 1933), p. 94.

12. Marjorie Fiske, *Middle Age: The Prime of Life?* (New York: Harper and Row, 1979), p. 83.

13. John Shea, *Stories of God: An Unauthorized Biography* (Chicago: Thomas More Press, 1978), pp. 43-44.

14. Johannes Metz, *The Advent of God* (New York: Newman Press, 1970), p. 27.

15. Eugene Gendlen, *Focusing* (New York: Everest House, 1978), p. 60.

16. Gould, *Transformations: Growth and Change in Adult Life*, p. 314.

17. Barbara Fried, *The Middle Age Crisis* (New York: Harper and Row, 1976), p. 95.

18. Karl Rahner, *Foundations of Christian Faith* (New York: Seabury Press, 1978), p. 432.

19. Gen. 1:3.

20. Gen. 1:31.

21. Matt. 10:30.

22. John 15:4.

23. John 14:9.

24. St. John of the Cross, *Dark Night of the Soul*, trans. E. Allison Peers (New York: Image Books, 1959), p. 100.

25. Bernard Lonergan, *Method in Theology* (New York: Herder and Herder, 1972), p. 242.

26. William Johnston, *The Inner Eye of Love* (San Francisco: Harper and Row, 1978), p. 146.

27. Gen. 1:27.

28. Rom. 8:35-39.

29. Karl Rahner, *Foundations of Christian Faith*, p. 432.

30. Col. 1:15-22.

31. Deut. 1:32.

32. Adrian Van Kaam, *The Transcendent Self* (Denville, N.J.: Dimension Books, 1979), p. 183.

33. John S. Dunne, *Time and Myth* (Notre Dame, Ind.: Notre Dame Press, 1973), p. 86.

34. Van Kaam, *The Transcendent Self*, p. 186.

35. William J. Fulco, *Maranatha, Reflections on the Mystical Theology of John the Evangelist* (New York: Paulist Press, 1973), p. 89.

36. Bernard Lonergan, *Method in Theology* (New York: Herder and Herder, 1972), p. 237.

37. Gould, Transformations: *Growth and Change in Adult Life*, p. 294.

38. Luke 23:34.

39. Luke 24:26.

40. John A. T. Robinson, *The Human Face of God* (Philadelphia: Westminister Press, 1973), p. 158.

# 3

# Insights for Mid-life Tasks and Spirituality: Jungian Personality Theory

ooking at the four seasons of a person's life span and sensing and experiencing that each season has its own particular joys and sorrows, its own particular tasks, its own contribution to the development and flowering of the human personality, one can be overcome with awe at the depth and design of the development of the human person. For Carl Jung, the development and flowering of the psyche (his word for personality) did not cease at childhood or young adulthood but continued throughout the person's lifetime. The particular joys, sorrows, and tasks of the four seasons of life that make up the development and flowering of the personality suggest a unique spirituality for each season. The spirituality of the season enfleshes and acts out the significance or goal of the season. Spirituality is the style in which we live out and express that which gives us meaning at the time.

At this moment in our culture, we have clearly defined the tasks of childhood and youth. The culture and the adults surrounding the person in these two stages of life fairly well define those tasks, allow for unique development, set clearly defined expectations, and give comparative assistance, support, and allowance of time for their accomplishment. We give the child leisure and freedom of responsibility. We encourage play and foster the child's unique personality. We develop responsibility slowly and developmentally. We encourage development in relationships and intellectual growth, not in an overbearing way, but rhythmically, almost watching in surprise what will unfold, while always evoking and stimulating. We have expectations for each year—3, 6, 9, 14, 18, 21, 30—and still we modulate our expectations according to the uniqueness of the person.

The ego development of the child and youth, hopefully, is a genuine development, true to the personality; yet we must realize that it is also a development of accommodation. Our culture stresses the rational over the affective and intuitive, the intellectual over the emotional, and extroverted qualities over introverted qualities. The child responds to fit into the expectations of society. Parents, friends, schools, media, churches, heroes, governments, institutions, and movements of all kinds make up the outer environment of the child and youth. Jung realized that the child's personality development is not formed by a partnership of the inner and outer world, but leans heavily toward the side of being dictated by the outer world. According to Jung, the primary task of the first half of life is the development of the ego, accommodating oneself to the external environment of home, school, friends, and society in general. We all know the joys and sorrows this entails: making the basketball team or not making it; being head of the class or being just mediocre; winning parental approval and affection or being denied it; making friends and being popular or always being on the left foot; developing gifts and talents or never knowing one has any; developing a strong self-image or suffering feelings of inferiority; having a strong sense of vocation or having no sense of it at all; reaching a flowering femininity or masculinity, or never having a definite, positive sexuality differentiation. For some, these tasks come easily; for others, there is an intense struggle. But eventually adolescents enter young adulthood knowing who they are, what kind of people or friends they prefer, what kind of work they like to do, and how they want to live (relationships and life-styles). It seems at times that all of this has been freely chosen and that the psychic rebirth that occurred with the movement from childhood to youth in the transition of adolescence was the becoming of an adult and the full flowering of the personality.

It is only in this century that we have clearly defined the developmental stages of the first half of life and realized that they are the necessary but only provisional stages of full human development. The full development and the flowering of the genuine Self remains for the second half of life. The psychic rebirth of the adolescent transition is a minor task in comparison to the psychic rebirth of the mid-life transition. For Jung, the rebirth of the mid-life transition is

> a long, drawn-out process of inner transformation and rebirth
> into another being. This "other being" is the other person in
> ourselves—that larger and greater personality maturing within us,
> whom we have already met as the inner friend or the soul. . . .
> The transformation processes strive to approximate them to one
> another, but our consciousness is aware of resistances, because
> the other person seems strange and uncanny, and because we
> cannot get accustomed to the idea that we are not absolute master
> in our own house. We should prefer always to be "I" and nothing
> else. But we are confronted with that inner friend or foe, and
> whether he is our friend or foe depends on ourselves.[1]

If the transition is made in the second half of life, the culture
and external environment play a minor role, if any role at all. Here,
accommodation to the outer environment is lowest on the list. During
the crisis and transition time the ego is in continual conflict with
the Self and rebirth is a gradual wedding of the conscious and the
unconscious, creating a union with differentiation. This is a lonely
time, solitary moments piled up, a spirituality dictated from the
depths of the psyche, a struggle and a warfare, a tearing and a
wrenching, a loving and a hating, a despair and a hope, a letting
go and a holding on, a death and a rebirth, a sameness and a newness, that no one can escape unless he or she deny him- or herself
entrance into the second half of life, and thus the continual, ongoing creation of the Self.

Whereas accommodation was the key word for the tasks of the
first half of life, individuation is the key word for the second half
of life. Although individuation is a natural process, integral to personal growth and psychic and spiritual wholeness, our culture and
society does not foster it; rather, it almost denies it, and therefore
makes the way even more difficult. Jung, speaking of this present
cultural phenomenon, wrote:

> Wholly unprepared, they embark upon the second half of life. Or
> are there perhaps colleges for forty-year-olds which prepares them
> for their coming life and its demands as the ordinary colleges
> introduce our young people to a knowledge of the world and of
> life? Thoroughly unprepared we take the step into the afternoon
> of life; worse still, we take this step with the false presumption that

our truths and ideals will serve us as hitherto. But we cannot live
the afternoon of life according to the programme of life's morning—for what was great in the morning will be little at evening,
and what in the morning was true will at evening become a lie.[2]

Then Jung goes on to point a finger at the churches for their contribution to the failure of the culture to evoke and foster full human
development.

> I said just now that we have no schools for forty-year-olds. That is
> not quite true. Our religions were always such schools in the past,
> but how many people regard them as such today? How many of us
> older persons have really been brought up in such a school and
> prepared for the second half of life, for old age, death and eter-
> nity?[3]

There is a beauty and integrity about each stage. There is a
beauty and integrity about the development of the ego in the first
half of life. Without it our culture could not survive; neither could
the individual. Yet the ego, as important as it is, is only a *part* of the
Self. This is central to Jung's personality theory. It is his major contribution to the development of self-understanding. We can com-
pare it to the discovery of America. Some had imagined and intuited land beyond the horizon, while others saw the same horizon
as a destructive end. It can be compared to our exploration of unknown space, the gradual revelation of what is out there affecting
us and determining us without our even knowing it. It can be compared to the sexual awakening of a person to the mystery of his or
her own body, desires, and needs, and to the complementarity of
another human body.

The mid-life transition, according to Jung, shifts the center of
gravity of the personality from the ego to the Self. "It is as though
the ego were the earth, and it suddenly discovered that the sun (or
the Self) was the centre of the planetary orbits and of the earth's or-
bit as well."[4]

It is not a case of demeaning the tasks and accomplishments of
the first half of life nor of despising the spirituality of youth that
flows from these tasks. It is a case of realizing that when they are accomplished, there is a whole new set of tasks to fulfill and they may
be in direct opposition to those of the first half of life. It is a case of

being awakened to the new tasks and being empowered from within with the courage needed to embark on this second journey. Both do not happen simultaneously. Depression, despondency, moodiness, restlessness, etc., come upon us and settle into us, and we experience a letdown at the accomplishments we worked so hard for. What got us up and going and filled us with zeal now leaves us empty and motionless. We have no idea, image or concept of the Self. We are not yet attuned to its messages. We are called to leave behind what has given us meaning and defined us in order to go out into the dark with faith that there is more to us. At this time our spirituality is letting go, accepting, living through and in this new experience, painful as it is. This inner prodding is the sign, the message of the unconscious.

Jung clearly speaks about the goals of the two distinct halves of life:

> It is highly important for a young person who is still unadapted and has as yet achieved nothing to shape the conscious ego as effectively as possible—that is, to educate the will. Unless he [or she] is positively a genius he even may not believe in anything active within himself that is not identical with his will. He must feel himself a man of will, and he may safely deprecate everything else within himself or suppose it subject to his will—for without this illusion he can scarcely bring about a social adaptation.

> It is otherwise with the person in the second half of life who no longer needs to educate his conscious will, but who, to understand the meaning of his individual life, must learn to experience his own inner being. Social usefulness is no longer an aim for him, although he does not question its desirability. Fully aware as he is of the social unimportance of his creative activity, he looks upon it as a way of working out his own development and thus benefiting himself. These last achievements in turn serve to further the patient in his social existence. For an inwardly sound and self-confident person will be more adequate to his social tasks than one who is not on good terms with his unconscious.[5]

Comparatively speaking, the individual's ego is made in the image and likeness of society. This ego has a great contribution to make. But the unique gift of the Self, the transcendence of society, a cultural breakthrough in the continual re-creation of the culture will take place only if the ego of the person lets go of the reins and enters into a relationship with the unconscious. This is the pre-requisite for the emergence of the genuine Self and the making of the individual into the image and the likeness of the Spirit of God. The spirituality of mid-life flows from the tasks of mid-life. It is objectively characterized in Jungian terms as inwardness, individuation, self-realization, integration, reconciliation, coming to self-hood. The means are subjectively unique to each person, as salvation for one is damnation for another. The end may be the same, but the means are as unique and variable as the individuals. "A solution which would be out of the question for me may be just the right one for someone else."[6]

It is a difficult task for those of us who equate the ego with the Self—and who does not fit into this category? The fact that the Self is comprised of the conscious self (ego) and the unconscious self is for many a shattering experience. Yet for others it becomes a liberating fact. Although at first the conscious and unconscious appear to be at odds with each other (sometimes even mortal enemies), in fact they are necessary and glorious parts of the whole, creating a genuine Self, a true personality:

> . . . Conscious and unconscious are not necessarily in opposition to one another, but complement one another to form a totality, which is the self. According to this definition the self is a quantity that is supraordinate to the conscious ego. It embraces not only the conscious but also the unconscious psyche, and is therefore, so to speak, a personality which we also are.[7]

The depression so characteristic of the mid-life crisis must be accepted and entered into. What is this that I am experiencing? Where does it come from? What is it telling me? A sense that there is more to me than I have experienced and a sense of an inner awakening will usher in the unseating of the ego, the conscious self. It is dethroned. This brings about violent repercussions. The ego has been god. It thought it was the Self. The danger lies not only in our failure to unseat the ego but the danger of allowing it to be replaced by the unconscious and allowing the unconscious to become our new god. Individuation calls for the gradual emergence of the unconscious and the necessary interaction of conscious and unconscious. This integration allows the Self to be in charge, dealing harmoniously with the conscious and unconscious aspects of Self. The period of midlife is often precipitated by an external and internal shift in our lives that thrusts us into our mid-life crisis or mid-life invitation. For Jung, that invitation was precipitated by his break with his friend and colleague, Sigmund Freud. "After the parting of the ways with Freud, a period of uncertainty began for me. It would be no exaggeration to call it a state of disorientation. I felt totally suspended in mid-air, for I had not yet found my own footing."[8]

Today we have a great deal more information about our anatomy then we do about our mind and spirit. Most children can name the internal and external parts of their bodies and describe their function, care, diseases, and cures. True, we have much more to learn, but we are far advanced in comparison to a comparable popular understanding of our psyche. The current trend toward holistic medicine and holistic living is sorely hampered by an ignorance of the essential parts of the psyche. We can all use atoms and molecules to describe what is scientifically invisible but we cannot generally do the same for our psyche, our life principle, our soul, our spirit.

When Jung speaks of the conscious self he is speaking of what you and I know of ourselves. I am woman-man, theist-atheist, industrious-lazy, friendly-unfriendly, pragmatist-dreamer, idealist-realist, honest-dishonest, good-bad, trustworthy-untrustworthy, etc. I have named myself doctor, mother, lawyer, husband, sensualist, friend, puritan, rapist, teacher, priest, minister, visionary, radical, traditionalist. This is my ego. This is what I have carved out of my unconscious for myself. It comprises the aspects of myself that I know. (What the ego does not know is that the opposite of many of these traits and aspects of the person are as much a part of the personality as the ego, but unconscious at this time.) It is not that the ego is not the true personality. It is possible, however, that some aspects of the ego could well be false to the person, as in the case of a profession to which the person is really ill suited.

Jung used the word *persona* to elucidate an aspect of the Self that carries the primary adaptive function of the individual and the function of the individual and the world. The persona is a part of the ego that is split off from the cluster of the conscious self (the ego). It could be a trait or a profession. People can be the motherly or fatherly type without necessarily being a biological mother or father. The mother or father image may consume them. Unknowingly they play a role into which their personality is assumed. The image of mother or father defines them. Others may be doctors or teachers and equate the role with their total personhood. They are teacher in their self-image. They present "teacher" to all the world, even the intimate spheres.

The persona is a mask. It originates in the collective unconscious. It is acceptable to society. I relate in every situation through this mask, and it makes relating easy and free from conflict. People need not encounter other aspects of me, so I do not have to deal with them or present them to the world. As far as I am concerned, they do not even exist. This identification is so tight that it is unconscious. There is no differentiation as there is, for example, with a new biological mother who knows she is truly mother but experiences this in conjunction with her other identities: child, lover, designer, daughter, etc. A differentiated man will experience fatherhood as an integral part of his ego, yet different from other aspects of his ego.

People in the second half of life are called to unseat the ego. But some cannot enter into that process unless they face the fact that they have been denying whole aspects of their own ego in allowing one or another aspect of it to usurp the whole conscious personality by taking on a superior and total role. Speaking of the difference between the terms *ego* and *persona*, Jung said:

> Well, you see, the ego is supposed to be the real representative of the real person. For instance, in the case where B knows of A, but A doesn't know of B, one would say the ego is more on the side of B, because the ego has a more complete knowledge and A is a split-off personality.[9]

Often we present a mask to other people. It is often a healthy and good thing to do. A man presents the mask of a doctor to his patients, a parent the mask of mother or daddy to a young child. When we know what we are doing, when we can differentiate the conscious aspects of ourself, when we are not equating this image with Self, we are wearing a mask or persona that facilitates and names the relationship at the moment. The inability to wear or assume a mask at times can be an unhealthy thing for ourselves and others.

Individuation is impossible without exposing and dissolving an inflated persona and dethroning the ego. The unconscious Self, the Self that lies deep within us, is demanding emergence, and unification with the ego is the ideal. This crisis time, like all crises, points to the fact that things can go either of two ways. We can come through the crisis and go forth on the path of becoming our true Self or we can end the crisis by regressing and putting the conscious personality securely on the throne again. This is the "self" we are familiar with. The devil we know, it seems, is better than the devil we do not know. If we succeed in dethroning the ego, we enter into a period of personality disorientation. We move from knowing who we think we are to not knowing who we are at all. We move from clear and definite goals to no goals. Jung wrote of this period:

> A collapse of the conscious attitude is no small matter. It always feels like the end of the world, as though everything had tumbled back into original chaos. One feels delivered up, disoriented, like a rudderless ship that is abandoned to the moods of the elements. So at least it seems.[10]

We can here give in to the collective in one of two ways: first, by returning to the upstaged persona or ego and alienating ourself from the true Self, thus surrendering to the collective approval our persona or ego has already won; or second, by replacing the ego control with the control of the unconscious, which is another form of collective control. This is another form of alienation from the Self because it involves a surrender to the undifferentiated collective images or archetypes that make up the structural content of the nonpersonal unconscious. Jung offers a happy solution to this dilemma: "The aim of individuation is nothing less than to divest the self of the false wrappings of the persona on the one hand, and of the suggestive power of the primordial images on the other."[11]

Our unconscious reaches back to our personal history (personal unconscious) and the past history of the human race (collective unconscious). This unconscious is also our psyche. Jung realized that our psyche produces images that have no connection to our personal history or experience but are rooted in the history and experience of all humanity. "Although we human beings have our own personal life, we are yet in large measure the representatives, the victims and promoters of a collective spirit whose years are counted in centuries."[12] Many of these images are of a religious content and so Jung saw the human psyche as religious by nature.

The reawakening and acceptance of the spiritual as integral to our nature became for Jung a keynote of the cure of souls and the healing of the culture. For Jung, the spiritual renewal of the person was most pressed for during the time of mid-life transition. In fact, the crisis of mid-life addresses the question: Will the spiritual renewal take place? Commenting on this aspect, Aniela Jaffe says, "It also became apparent to him [Jung] that numerous neuroses spring from a disregard for this fundamental [spiritual] characteristic of the psyche, especially during the second half of life."[13]

Jung seldom wrote about his own personal unconscious, but in Memories, Dreams, Reflections we read, "My life is a story of the self-realization of the unconscious. Everything in the unconscious seeks outward manifestation, and the personality too desires to evolve out of its unconscious conditions and to experience itself as whole."[14] But self-knowledge and self-realization demand courage and the emergence of the unconscious demands fortitude and an attitude of respect. Jung's split with Freud, which cost him the loss of all his friends and acquaintances, ushered him into a long transition period where he wrestled fiercely but reverently with his unconscious.

A turning point in this transition of seven to ten years came as a result of a series of dreams. He records for us the meaning of a significant dream:

> "Why, that is the problem that is being played out in the world." Siegfried, I thought, represents what the Germans want to achieve, heroically to impose their will, have their own way. "Where there is a will there is a way!" I had wanted to do the same. But now that was no longer possible. The dream showed that the attitude embodied by Siegfried, the hero, no longer suited me. Therefore it had to be killed.

> After the deed I felt an overpowering compassion, as though I my-self had been shot; a sign of my secret identity with Siegfried, as well as the grief a man feels when he is forced to sacrifice his ideal and his conscious attitude. This identity and my heroic idealism had to be abandoned, for there are higher things than the ego's will, and to these one must bow.[15]

As the dream reached its conclusion, a tremendous downfall of rain came. Reflecting on this, Jung sensed that he was drawing near the end of his crisis and transition. "The rain showed that the tension between consciousness and the unconscious was being resolved."[16] The transcendent function was at work. The emergence of the Self was becoming reality for Jung. From childhood he had contact with this personality, which he called the Number Two Personality. But he could not integrate it with his ego self. He had to let it be, lying dormant as it seemed, during the first half of life. During this period Jung never let go of his ego self. ". . . At this time . . . I needed a point of support in 'this world,' and I may say that my family and my professional work were that to me. It was most essential for me to have a normal life in the real world as a counterpoise to that strange inner world."[17] Still, he made great adjustments in his life to accommodate himself in this turning point and to respond to the feelings of disorientation that beseiged him. He developed a new attitude toward his patients. He comforted himself with the realization that his very strength as a healer came from his weakness, his own wounds. Jung's relationship with his patients reflects his attitude: "Only if the doctor knows how to cope with himself and his own problems will he be able to teach the patient to do the same."[18] "The doctor is effective only when he himself is affected. Only the wounded physician heals."[19] The "constant inner pressure" that he experienced during this time of turmoil encouraged him to return to his own personal history and childhood memories. From within his personal unconscious came the image of a ten- and eleven-year-old passionately building with blocks, then stone and mud. He had contacted the creative child within himelf that could help to unlock the creative unconscious and the key to the Self that was trembling to be reborn. Jung actually gave vent to this child and allowed himself the leisure to play at building in hopes of facilitating a new birth.

> I went on with my building game after the noon meal every day, whenever the weather permitted. As soon as I was through eating, I began playing, and continued to do so until the patients arrived; and if I finished my work early in the evening, I went back to building. In the course of this activity my thoughts clarified, and I was able to grasp the fantasies whose presence in my life I dimly felt. . . . I was on the way to discovering my own myth."[20]

All of this self-help and therapy demanded a commitment of time and energy on Jung's part. He temporarily put aside the continuation of his academic career as professor in order to devote time to the discovery of this "pearl of great price." This cost him dearly, but the sting of the deprivation wore off under his giving in to the demands of his inner personality.

Around 1918–1919, seven years after his break with Freud, Jung gradually came to the end of the darkness of his crisis-transition. Coming to terms with what he called his anima and the therapeutic activity of his own mandala drawings facilitated and empowered another crucial turning point. Jung was reaching one of the crucial moments of individuation. He had remained faithful to the Self by dethroning but not shipwrecking his ego and by faithfully dealing with every signal of his unconscious while not letting it rule or dominate him. In reality, our ego is formed out of our unconscious. But the Self wants to maintain a living relationship with the ego and the unconscious. The ego tends to believe that it is the entire Self, and at the time of mid-life crisis to persist in identifying the ego with the Self means spiritual suicide, death to the personality and to continual becoming. Closure occurs at this point — and unless it is reversed, there is no possibility of wholeness or self-realization.

In order for us to understand the anima that Jung experienced both within and outside himself and to reflect upon the anima or animus within and without each of us, we will first look at the dynamic content of the unconscious which Jung calls archetypes. We all have an intuitive sense about instincts. We acknowledge that each bird has an in-built pattern that unconsciously directs it to the building of a nest. Archetypes are similar in-built patterns that are part of our psyche and direct and regulate the personality of each individual in a unique way. The bird is not free to choose whether to build the nest. In the same way we are not free to choose whether to evoke the archetypes. They are autonomous personalities, a part of our unconscious that demands an entrance into our personality. If we cooperate with that entrance and allow the conscious and the unconscious to relate, the aspects of the archetypes will have a creative and beneficial influence on our personality development. If not, the same archetypes will have their way — they will enter into our personality development but in a harmful and destructive way. "The archetypal structure elements of the psyche are psychic organs upon whose functioning the well-being of the individual depends, and whose injury has disastrous consequences."[21] Within each of us in what we are calling the unconscious are patterns of behavior, patterns of being and doing that lie dormant and unconscious, wanting and needing to be activated. Our goal is that they should be not only activated but in some glorious way integrated into the conscious.

Think of all the ways of being and doing that the history of the human race attributes to being man or being woman. These are the inherited, archetypal, structural components of the psyche. Originally, Jung saw the feminine archetypal pattern (which he called the *anima*) in every man and the corresponding masculine archetypal pattern (the *animus*) in every woman. The first half of life gives us the time to develop our masculinity or femininity, and the opposite within us (the anima or animus) is content to let the ego develop that way. But as we move into midlife, there is a necessity and compulsion to give the dormant and now restless archetypal pattern an opportunity to be activated and integrated. If the ego is challenged, it will unconsciously resist this display of the anima or animus that contradicts its attitude. If we do not sense and allow the archetypal patterns to come to consciousness, the ego will force its way in demonic forms. One marriage I know was redeemed after the unconscious anima was recognized by a man, the father of seven girls, married twenty-five years and the holder of two full-time jobs as professor and construction worker. He needed the work to support his family according to the demands of his ego; he also loved the work, as it filled his mind and body with the enthusiasm of a creator and prevented him from the possibility of any close, stifling relationship. The need to work for a large family meant no vacations, no dinners out, no leisurely moments together. The pain of a strained relationship of twenty-five years and daughters leaving the home so well provided for materially cracked open the masculine heart and ego to allow the womanly part of him, his yearning for relationship, his yearning for softness, its well-deserved and long-awaited entrance. Will his masculine ego be dissolved? No. But it will be affected and he will have an inkling that there is a whole other person, a stranger to himself, waiting for him to get to know.

Much of the moodiness and depression in a mid-life crisis is caused by the revolt of the anima or animus. "They personify the collective unconscious, and therefore their true psychological purpose is to be a function of relationship between the ego and the collective unconscious to build a bridge, as it were, between the world of consciousness and the world of inner images."[22] Unless the anima or animus comes to some conscious activation, we will not be able to differentiate either and we will fall into their uncontrolled power. The worse characteristics of the male or female will be unconsciously acted out in us. We can go for blood tests and be told that we have too much of one thing in our blood and not enough of another. We can regulate and control this by diet and chemicals. It is not quite as easy with our psyche and archetypal patterns. We know when we don't have enough fresh air or exercise but we don't know when we are lacking in the exercise of the archetypal patterns of feminine or masculine being and doing and psychic meaning. Have I realized the exercise of caring for someone or something simply because they are in need and without looking for a reward? Have I exercised the power to relate to someone intimately and passionately and given the relationship the top priority of mutal companionship? Have I exercised the pattern in me that must allow me to be solitary, to find my own space and drink in my nourishment from the impersonal cosmos, and/or dedicate myself, unhampered by another, to the work I see before me? Have I allowed the wise woman within me to contact the needs of others and the needs of the coming age and forget the private domain long enough to be a visionary and give birth to new creative ideas? All these patterns are part of my own human equipment and desire acceptance. It is not a matter of willpower or intellectual consent. It is a matter of paying attention to the irrational movements in myself and looking for their identity and then accepting and affirming these seemingly foreign strangers in myself. I begin to allow the Self to repattern me. What I am discovering seems incompatible not only with my self-image or ego but with each other. The transcendent function is the baby maker. It allows the miracle of integration to take place and eventually I give birth to a more genuine Self.

There are other patterns more typically masculine or animus style in comparison to the four feminine or anima patterns mentioned above. There is the pattern of the youth, doing and creating a million projects and jumping from one to the other in a fascinating way, always busy and engaged. There is within you the pattern of a hero, defiant and assertive for the good despite the consequences. The pattern of a father is in you, allowing you to logically and skillfully direct and guide yourself and others along the right way. The possibility of transpersonal love is yours. It can direct you to point the way to others, to set their hearts on fire, and to be consumed in a holy love. These patterns of human behavior are our inheritance. Our ego may represent some of them, but we regard the others as scapegoats. They want and need to be accepted and our wholeness is dependent upon this. Jung's original idea that the woman had to activate the animus and the man the anima has been developed in these past decades to allow us to realize that many men and women are ego-identified with only one or more of the archetypal patterns of their sexual identification. Therefore, we can activate any of these patterns, masculine and feminine, that have not been acknowledged, transformed, and integrated. "Masculine traits can also be part of the nonpersonal unconscious potential in men and be obsessive, animus fashion; so can feminine traits in women. Instinct, soul and spirit, anima and animus are archetypal principles that pertain to both sexes equally."[23]

Sometimes I think we are all like a baby grand piano. The Self is the pianist and composer as well as the composition. Within the Self is the archetypal pattern of wholeness that is played out as the Self composes and plays the keys of the myriad of archetypal patterns. Half notes, whole notes, a rest here and there, the composition rings out a unique, one-of-a-kind creation. While the archetypal structures in all of us are the same, like the internal structure of the baby grand piano, the pattern of wholeness within us is an arrangement and a Self that is as unique as our fingerprints, unmatched in the history of the human race.

If inwardness and becoming our own true Self is the task of mid-life, then our spirituality is cut out for us. We must let the pattern of wholeness emerge in our mid-life experience. We must let the unconscious and inner life take precedence. We must discover the ways that will lead to self-knowledge and self-realization.

What is spirituality? It is the spilling out of an inner reality. It is the incarnation of a spirit. In the first half of life our spirituality flowed from how we perceived ourself and other things. It flowed out of our ego, our consciousness. If we look at where we put our psychic energy we discover our values, what is of prime importance to us, what sets our spirits on fire, and how we enact or incarnate that spirit. We discover our spirituality.

Jung saw the redirection of psychic energy from the outer world to the inner world as the primary shift that occurs in mid-life transition.

Ira Progoff describes for us what a creative person does when he or she comes to an impasse in his or her work. It appears that the same can be said about people undergoing mid-life crisis if they too release their creativity. In mid-life crisis we have come to an impasse in our work. A style of being, working, and developing has accomplished the developmental personality task for the first half of life, adaptation to the outer world. The creative question is: What now? Progoff says that when the impasse is reached:

> It is time for him [or her] to do some research into [him- or herself]. This means turning his attention inward, and to take such a step is often exceedingly difficult for the person who has been accustomed to directing his energies entirely outward. The inner world often seems unreal to such a person, especially in his first contacts with it; but he soon is able to realize that it is real indeed, especially when he perceives that it is, and always has been, the instigator and secret director of his outer activities.[24]

One begins to sense that the Self (or what Jung also called the Number Two Personality) is a friend that has been with us all along, directing us and waiting for this second half of life for the real unfolding, the full flowering.

Our primary concern in the second half of life is the fulfillment of the personality that is closest to us—our own. It is the part of creation for which we are primarily responsible. Although the spirituality of each person in mid-life will be tailored to his or her own uniqueness, there are basic qualities or directions that most mid-life spiritualities will incorporate.

Uniqueness is the primary characteristic. It prompted Jung to recall this ancient saying: "If the wrong man uses the right means, the right means works in the wrong way."[25] This uniqueness is emphasized in the inwardness that is developed as the person takes the time to grow in self-knowledge and to allow the kingdom within to be set in order and the true Self to emerge. Inwardness endorses a reverence for Self even as the person encounters his or her shadow. The shadow is the archetypal image that Jung used to name all the aspects of Self that have been repressed or suppressed because they are the opposite of the honored ego traits that have been nurtured, or the opposite of the typology that has been most comfortable, or the parts of the individual that most resemble our prehistoric ancestors. When I realize the universal character of my shadow, it releases me to accept it with its many faces and even to embrace them. Such acceptance and embracing releases the transcendent function to negotiate some kind of rapprochement with the conscious ego and I become humbled. I accept the shady side of my own person and my humble beginnings and I become more tolerant of those who find themselves in the grip of their shadow. I discover my commonality with all people. I realize what my humanity means. Not only do I incorporate in myself all the shadow or unacceptable aspects of being human, but all the glorious ones too.

> It is more than knowing that one belongs to the same species as other [people]. It is knowing that there is something within one-self corresponding to whatever one finds in other [people]. It is actually feeling and acknowledging the resonance within oneself to what-ever one meets in others. It is thus a very vivid realization of one's own humanity and theirs.[26]

We must remember the image of creation that is so familiar to us but whose significance we often forget. God made us out of the dust of the earth and breathed into us God's own life. "The unconscious extends into the lower layer of man's animal nature and it also reaches up, out and beyond the merely human toward a meaningful contact with the infinite aspects of life."[27] Because of this we must not only speak of the depths of the psyche but also of the magnitude and height of the psyche.

Coming to terms with our shadow gives us an appreciation for our past and all the archetypes. We realize that today is the result of yesterday.

> No matter how much we are today, there has been a yesterday, which was just as real, just as human and warm as the moment we call Now, which—helas—in a few hours will be a Yesterday as dead as the first of January Anno Domini 1300. A good half of the reasons why things now are what they are is buried in Yesterday.[28]

Our psyche is made up of our personal yesterday and the yesterday of the prehistoric ages. The mid-life person incorporates into his or her personality acceptance of the personal and nonpersonal past. This is done by giving time to recall that personal story and history. We discover in our personal unconscious the events and people who have helped to make us who we are today.

Dreams, daydreams, imaginations, fantasies, art works, journals, dialogues with personifications of our archetypes, doodling, slips of the tongue, projections, prayer, and even complexes and neuroses can all be means by which we can contact our unconscious and the present unfolding of the Self as well as obtain a hint of the future Self. Jung spent hours at creative play and active imagination during the time of his mid-life transition. Mandala drawings entered significantly into the resolution of his conscious and unconscious self. The mandalas were portraits of his inner Self. The mandala drawings reflected the production of a new center of personality. "The true mandala is always an inner image, which is gradually built up through (active) imagination, at such times when psychic equilibrium is disturbed or when a thought cannot be found and must be sought for."[29]

It appears to us that our unconscious is a mass of patterns of being and acting that have no order or hierarchy. The mandala unfolds the order of the unconscious and allows us to discover the center of the psyche, the Self. Here with the genuine Self we discover the primary myth of our life. "All life is bound to individual carriers who realize it, and it is simply inconceivable without them. But every carrier is charged with an individual destiny and destination, and the realization of these alone makes sense of life."[30] Unknown to us, the Self has been guiding us all along the way and now in mid-life it reverses position with the ego. The Self becomes the center of the personality. This is the major conversion of mid-life. From it flows our unique spirituality, faithful to the Self and the myth of our personal story. This is the crisis of mid-life: Can I redirect my psychic energies and discover my true Self?

Reflecting on mid-life, William Johnston writes:

> Jung had a real insight into the religious dimension of this great crisis. I believe that in this psychological turmoil grace is working gently, if painfully, in the unconscious inviting our number two personality, our true selves, to emerge from the womb into fullness of life. Quite often the whole process of middle age crisis is nothing less than a mystical experience of death and resurrection to a new life which is filled with true joy.[31]

The spirituality of the second half of life incorporates reconciliation of the polarities of life: light and darkness, death and resurrection, male and female, good and evil. "The point is not conversion into the opposites but conservation of previous values together with recognition of their opposite."[32]

It is within our unconscious that we discover the polarities and their mediating function. "At the climateric . . . it is necessary to give special attention to the images of the collective unconscious, because they are the source from which hints may be drawn for the solution of the problem of opposites."[33]

A primary set of opposites is the body–spirit one. Jung writes:

> The attractive power of the pysche brings about a new self-estimation—a re-estimation of the basic facts of human nature. We can hardly be surprised if this leads to the rediscovery of the body after its long depreciation in the name of the spirit.[34]

We must rid ourselves of the anitithesis between mind and body.

> If we can reconcile ourselves with the mysterious truth that spirit is the living body seen from within and the body the outer manifestation of the living spirit—the two really being one—then we can understand why it is that the attempt to transcend the present level of consciousness must give its due to the body. We shall also see that belief in the body cannot tolerate an outlook that denies the body in the name of the spirit.[35]

Mid-life spirituality will incorporate a wholistic approach to the human person and reverence of the body, sexuality, and bodily needs.

Mid-life spirituality flows out of a free and loving acceptance of our own uniqueness, the secret of our own personality and fidelity to it. This secret is found in the true Self, our own unique patterning of the conscious and unconscious forces of our own personality. It directs us to set out on a second journey that is created and designed by the Self. This journey or way of life reflects more readily the true Self, while not neglecting the ego, and fosters the continual becoming of the Self. If all of this rings true to you, seems right from within, illuminates your experience, gives you faith, hope, and love in your past, present, and future, and integrates your fragmented sections, then Carl Jung deserves the thanks. He said of himself, "My life has been permeated and held together by one idea and one goal: namely, to penetrate into the secret of the personality. Everything can be explained from this central point, and all my works relate to this one theme."[36] This was his own personal myth. Because of it we too have been helped to discover our own myths. Like Jesus, our mid-life spirituality requires that we sell everything for the pearl of great price, for the truth of our own inner wisdom.

"Imitation of Christ . . . might be taken as the duty to give reality
to one's best conviction, always the fullest expression of individual
temperament, with the same courage and the same self-sacrifice
shown by Jesus."[37]

The inwardness of the mid-life person brings about a spirituality
that looks inward for its nourishment, renewal, and guidance. In
possession of itself, it looks outward to all of creation in transpersonal love, looking for its own unique way to respond to the challenge. "The gift you have received give as a gift."[38]

## Notes

1. C. G. Jung, *Archetypes*, trans. A. F. C. Hull (Princeton: Princeton
University Press), 1959, pp. 64–65.

2. C. G. Jung, *Modern Man in Search of a Soul*, trans. W. S. Dell and
Gary F. Baynes (New York: Harcourt, Brace and World, 1933), p. 108.

3. *Ibid.*, p. 109.

4. *Ibid.*, p. 70.

5. *Ibid.*, pp. 70–71.

6. C. G. Jung, *Memories, Dreams, Reflections*, rev. ed. trans. Richard
and Clara Winston, ed. Aniela Jaffe (New York: Random House), 1961, p.
131.

7. C. G. Jung, *Two Essays on Analytical Psychology*, 2d ed., trans.
R. F. C. Hull (New York: Meridian Books, 1956), p. 178.

8. Jung, *Memories, Dreams, Reflections*, p. 170.

9. Richard I. Evans, *Jung on Elementary Psychology* (New York: E. P.
Dutton & Co., 1976), p. 81.

10. Jung, *Two Essays on Analytical Psychology*, p. 163.

11. *Ibid.*, p. 174.

12. Jung, *Memories, Dreams, Reflections*, p. 91.

13. *Ibid.*, p. x.

14. *Ibid.*, p. 3.

15. *Ibid.*, pp. 180–81.

16. *Ibid.*, p. 181.

17. *Ibid.*, p. 187.

18. *Ibid.*, p. 132.

19. *Ibid.*, p. 134.

20. *Ibid.*, pp. 174–75.

21. Erich Neumann, *The Origins and History of Consciousness*, trans.

R. F. C. Hull, Bollingen Series, no. 42 (Princeton: Princeton University Press, 1954), p. xv.

22. John A. Sanford, *Invisible Partners* (New York: Paulist Press, 1980), p. 64.

23. Edward C. Whitmont, "Reassessing Femininity and Masculinity: A Critique of Some Traditional Assumptions," in *Quadrant* 13:120.

24. Ira Progoff, *Depth Psychology and Modern Man* (New York: McGraw-Hill, 1973), p. 207.

25. C. G. Jung, *Psyche and Symbol,* ed. Violet S. de Laszlo (New York: Doubleday, 1958), p. 304.

26. John S. Dunne, *The Way of All the Earth* (New York: Macmillan Company, 1972), 220.

27. Ira Progoff, *Jung's Psychology and Its Social Meaning* (New York: Doubleday, 1973), pp. 249-50.

28. Jung, *Psyche and Symbol,* p. xiii.

29. C. G. Jung, "Dreams," trans. R. F. C. Hull in *Collected Works of C. G. Jung,* Bollingen Series, no. 20 (Princeton: Princeton University Press, 1959), p. 170.

30. *Ibid.,* p. 96.

31. William Johnston, *The Inner Eye of Love* (San Francisco: Harper and Row, 1978), p. 148.

32. Jung, *Two Essays on Analytical Psychology,* p. 76.

33. *Ibid.,* p. 109.

34. Jung, *Modern Man in Search of a Soul,* p. 219.

35. *Ibid.,* p. 220.

36. Jung, *Memories, Dreams, Reflections,* p. 206.

37. Jung, *Psyche and Symbol,* p. 349.

38. Matt. 10:8b.

# 4

# Mid-life Transition as Creation and Incarnation

## Creation

Yet, O Lord, you are our father; we are the clay and you the potter: we are all the work of your hands.[1]

This word came to Jeremiah from the Lord: Rise up, be off to the potter's house; there I will give you my message. I went down to the potter's house and there he was, working at the wheel. Whenever the object of clay which he was making turned out badly in his hand, he tried again, making of the clay another object of whatever sort he pleased. Then the word of the Lord came to me: Can I not do to you, house of Israel as this potter has done? says the Lord. Indeed, like clay in the hands of the potter so are you in my hand, house of Israel.[2]

These two jewels from the Hebrew Scriptures are set within the context of the deepest concern of the prophets, the setting of salvation: the conversion of the chosen people. The Isaiahs and Jeremiah were passionately calling Israel back to its true self, back to unadulterated monotheism. In each case the heart of what the prophet is talking about is God, "the Potter," perpetually saving God's own creation, God's own people, "the clay."

God took the red clay and breathed into it a living spirit. In the beginning, the image of the one gently kneading life- and breath-giver greets us in the Yahwist theologians' second chapter of Genesis. Humanity is represented by the clay. "That man is made of clay is a very old common idea in the Near East and

66

its origin correlates to that of the Potter."[3] Isaiah 29:16 and 45: 9 each refer to the Potter, Israel's God, the Lord of Creation beside whom there is no other. In all these places, it is presumed that the clay is involved in the process. The "clay" is not merely passive; it has freedom enough to dare to resist the work of the Potter while in reality its freedom is not for such resistance, but for co-creation.

In the parable in action from Jeremiah, it is the House of Israel that is being formed and reformed. Whenever the object of clay turns out badly, the Potter takes the same clay and remodels it. In the next few lines of the Jeremiah passage, in the same anthropomorphic way, the author has the Lord repenting of the evil he threatens to do to a nation when that nation turns from evil. The clay, Israel, in its freedom has certain power over the Potter and effects the remolding process. In this imagery we have a glimpse of the whole mystery of Creation. The artist knows its every movement. The artist has a vision and knows how to urge the ever-changing and often deviant process toward that vision to incorporate the vision into the process and even how to transform the deviations. This is a dynamic picture of the Creator at work and it is at one with a kind of creation story that not only illuminates the history of Israel but even a scientific evolutionary world view.

In its evocation of the image of the clay in Genesis, this story has the power to awaken in us an almost reflex association of fall/redemption. The fall/redemption version of the meaning of history has dominated Christian theology for many centuries. It rests on the vision of creation as complete and perfect "in the beginning." It presumes a static world view. It imposes on any idea of process a notion of restoration rather than one of ongoing creation.

> Whenever we talk about creation we instinctively think theologically about the original state of the world and the beginning of all things, imagining them as a condition that was once finished, complete and in itself, perfect.[4]

History is paradise lost and one long exile with redemption seen as a return "in the end" to the original lost condition of perfection. The pattern again turns up in the history of religions as the myth of the eternal return. In this case the return is, of course, paradise regained.

"Modern exegesis of the Old and New Testaments, however, will not allow us to maintain this notion of Creation."[5] This kind of traditional interpretation made creation seem to be outside history, a historical prehistory. The Fall seemed to be the beginning of history and the Abraham story the beginning of redemption or salvation history. Yet we recognize both the Priestly and Yahwist versions of creation (Genesis 1-2:4a and 2:4b-3:1 respectively) as literary distillations of what the chosen people came to believe about the origin of God's involvement in their salvation history. The Yahwist authors in about the ninth century B. C. and later the Priestly authors in about the seventh century B. C. captured the oral traditions about the creation, which were the theologizing of a people who had been saved over and over by their God. Israel had interpreted the exodus, the covenant, and the settlement of the promised land as salvation history. Yet Israel's entry into Palestine was one end of a series of events that began "in the beginning." "Presumptuous as it may sound, creation is part of the aetiology of Israel."[6] In both these documents, woven with others into what we know as the one book of Genesis, Yahweh's work of creation is not undertaken independently, but for the sake of Israel's history. Each story of creation is incorporated into a course of history leading from the beginning to the call of Abraham. It is to make the saving relationship granted by Yahweh to Israel legitimate that "both pictures of history start with the creation and from there they draw the line out toward themselves and toward Israel and the Tabernacle and the Promised Land."[7] By the time of these writings in the evolution of Israel's creed, the Creation itself was regarded as an integral part of all the saving work of God.

This means that for Israel, the Creation story was captured from the timeless world of other myths to be part of time and history itself. The process is even squeezed into a sequence of "days." Time and therefore change and so salvation began with creation. "But if creation is open to change from the beginning, then it cannot be a closed system; it must be an open one."[8] It is not circular, closing in on itself. In this view, then, the Bible does not present creation

ahistorically, nor the destiny of time and history as a turning back
to the static perfection of the beginning. Creation and salvation
almost coincide in the biblical view of reality and they move with
history forward in time. What then is the priestly point of God's
resting, or the Yahwist's future time of the universal fulfillment of
the blessing given to Abraham? What then is the goal of history? In
the biblical terms of the Christian Scriptures, it is eschatological.
The end time is when "God will be All in All."[9]

> It follows from this that theology must talk about creation not
> only at the beginning but also in history and at the end. . . . The
> reduction of the concept of creation to creation in the beginning
> has led traditionally either to the cleavage between creation and
> redemption and between nature and super-nature or to a divi-
> sion between the first and the second creation. But this calls into
> question the continuity and unity of the divine creative activity
> itself.[10]

In the beginning there was creation through God's bringing order
out of chaos. Yet the forces of chaos, night and sea, threaten and
encroach on creation throughout the course of history. It is only in
the apocalyptic vision of the end time that they are absent. "Then
I saw a new heaven and a new earth. The former heaven and the
former earth had passed away and the sea was no longer."[11] "The
night shall be no more. They will need no light from lamps or from
the sun. The Lord God shall give them light, and they shall reign
forever."[12] At that time there will be no more death and no more
weeping. On the personal level, night and the sea are presented in
images of death and tears.

In the Christian Scriptures, references to creation are obvious
in the passages about the lilies of the field and the birds of the
air. Yet, the less obvious though more powerful revelations about
creation are found at the heart of the Gospels. They are embed-
ded in the proclamations of resurrection and the indwelling of
the Spirit. Resurrection is God's saving and creative action in
Jesus and through him, in all of humanity. Resurrection becomes
a possibility for everyone. Resurrection means Christ alive and
intimately present within one's very self. "I live now not I," says
Paul, "but Christ lives in me." Resurrection means that through
the spirit of Christ, God cohabits in my own individuality. He is

the life-giving Spirit, making eternal life and the overcoming of death a human potential.

In the same reversal, creation's subjection to futility has been undone, for the world itself will be freed from its slavery to corruption. Resurrection has overcome not only death and weeping for humanity, but also the destruction and corruption of the creation of which we are an integral part.

> I consider the sufferings of the present time are not worth comparing with the glory about to be revealed to us. For the creation waits with eager longing for the revealing of the children of God; for the creation was subjected to futility, not of its own will but by the will of the one who subjected it, in hope that the creation itself will be set free from its bondage to decay and will obtain the freedom of the glory of the children of God. We know that the whole creation has been groaning in labor pains until now; and not only the creation but we ourselves; who have the first fruits of the Spirit, groan inwardly while we wait for adoption, the redemption of our bodies. For in hope we were saved. Now hope that is seen is not hope. For who hopes for what is seen?[13]

What a breakthrough such a hope is. The ability to even imagine such a freedom is a breakthrough.

Going back to the Potter's shed with Jeremiah, we can see again that any time the object of clay that he was making turned out badly he tried again, making of the clay another object. The Potter's creation is a series of transformations. The earth and its people are transformed again and again until there comes a psychic birth into corporate personality. The House of Israel had such a birth of corporate self-consciousness. In the corporate conventional conscious, "the individual is accorded worth because he belonged to a community, not because he was an individual as such."[14] The communal consciousness issues, vaguely at first in about the seventh century B.C., into an individual consciousness. In the Christian Scriptures, however, we see a whole new emphasis on the creation and re-creation of that individual as individual.[15] The process, a constant conversion, a death-resurrection, a dying and rebirth, becomes the ongoing creation of each individual.

With Jesus and Resurrection there is a shift from awareness of the Potter's forming of the House of Israel to the Potter's care and creation of the individual. With Christ, the doctrine of the Creation intensely becomes the ongoing creation of each individual. Here again, creation and salvation are coextensive.

With evolutionary theory, ongoing creation-salvation takes on an even more specific texture. Developmental psychology adds another dimension. Each person's process of creation is a progression resembling the physical and psychic mutations of the race as it evolved. From the womb on, not only do each person's cells divide and become more complex, but the psychic development also follows a similar complexification process. The theory of the similarity between the evolution of consciousness of the race and the development of individual consciousness has received support from the work of Erich Neumann. The study of the growth of consciousness or cognitive development of each individual is, of course, the legacy of Jean Piaget. Carl Jung's work and the work of other developmental psychologists verify such patterns in adults.

What does commitment to a doctrine of creation do to the process of the development of the individual and the race and what does this commitment do to that moment in the developmental process that is the mid-life transition?

To know oneself as in the hands of a Potter is to encounter oneself in a whole new way. It takes one beyond private needs, ambitions, drives, expectations. It situates one in a whole new horizon. It provides a context for one's whole life. It dignifies and affirms all one's strivings for growth. It is to find oneself within an ultimate meaning. How different this is from the need to absolutize one's own drives in order to give ultimate meaning to life. How different even from having to absolutize an abstract value.

With resurrection as part of one's horizon, not only is one in the hands of the Potter, but one is the very dwelling of God. Such intimacy does not destroy individuality, for this is the God who is love. The personal God is one who loves each îother.î Love is the only force that can create unity without destroying the uniqueness of individual things. Love unites while it further integrates. True love never annihilates the beloved. To be able to experience such a connectedness with a loving, transcendent other in the inward layers of one's being, to be able to conceive such a relationship as a personal possibility and to let oneself go in it, is to move beyond narcissism while enhancing individuality.

During the developmental process, this love may become a total preoccupation and so a kind of ego inflation, a defensiveness and self-adoration. Self-development and self-fulfillment factored to infinity creates an idol. It makes the Self an end and so closes the process in upon itself. The Self, even the quest to become one's own true Self by integrating the conscious and unconscious, can never become an idol. Even the archetype of the Self can consume one. In this case, what one is possessed by is, paradoxically, not the true Self.

The Judeo-Christian myth of creation expands the true Self to the infinite Other and all others. Held not only intellectually but affectively, it participates in the transformation into the true Self. The deeper one goes into the well of this Self, the more one comes to realize the underground stream where each of us is united to all others.[16] Knowing through resurrection that the Self is the locus of eternal life springing from the Infinite Other, one can relax in never plumbing the depths of the Self. One can relax and enjoy the process, which need not end in this life.

As mentioned, the Judeo-Christian myth of creation is a myth drawn back into time and geography. "Myth can attach itself to historical characters and events as much as those that are fabulous."[17] The same myth seems to have the power to keep one in touch with one's clay while at the same time catching one up into a "seventh heaven." If the psychological danger is inflation—to be eaten up by an archetype—the best protection is to be connected with one's wholeness, "most definitely including the dark and guilty limitations."[18] Creation as salvation keeps one in touch with one's dark side while it keeps one in touch with infinite, eternal potential.

In the mid-life transition, when one is drawn inward, when the process of the ego stops dead in apathy, monotony, bordeom, dawdling over tasks, when energy is withdrawn from the conscious, an overarching faith and trust in a process of ongoing creation can be a crucial new dimension. Clinging however feebly to a Creator, especially with such an image as the Potter, can sustain one. It can underpin the feeling of stagnation and death and help transform the process of decay into new growth. Ongoing creation will be moved forward by the hope of resurrection.

In the mid-life period, even in the midst of anger, fear, regret, or doubt, the person can have an ultimate Other to confront, be angry

with, and doubt if he or she has been swimming in a historically interpreted doctrine of Creation. Beyond this the regret and the fear are
eased in the intermittent moments of affective surrender to the "one who
goes before," the One who is intimately present to the self that holds all
one's potentials. To be created means that at the deepest level a person
derives his or her whole existence and activity from a Creator God. He
or she is, as it were, first of God and only in that and through that is
himself or herself. One's existence and life are grounded in God, one's
whole life is undergirded by the freedom of God who in a transcendent
fashion gives each man or woman himself or herself. He or she is a
person through the transcending, active immanence of God

As we negotiate the potentials of the Self, one by one, assaulted by
and befriending animus and anima, shadow, wisdom figure, child, or
any other aspect of the whole Self, we know with Paul that because
of the intimacy with the Risen One, nothing can ultimately harm
or annihilate us.

> Who will separate us from the love of Christ? Trial or distress or
> persecution or hunger, or nakedness or danger or the sword? As
> scripture says: for your sake we are being slain all the day long; we
> are looked upon as sheep to be slaughtered. Yet in all this we are
> more conquerors because of him who loved us. For I am certain
> that neither death nor life, neither angels nor principalities, nei-
> ther the present nor the future, nor powers, neither height nor
> depth nor any other creature will be able to separate us from the
> love of God that comes to us in Christ Jesus, our Lord.[20]

The questioning and crumbling of the outer structures of the first
half of life has a context of love. All the evils of the crisis and its prodding toward transition has a context of love. The life one lives, what
one does for love has eternal significance. Even the evil one does is
transformed in the context of a Lover/Creator and can be a source
of light, new life, and strength. As one goes through the stages of the
death of one's youth, creation becomes the context "that you may not
grieve as others do who have no hope."[21]

## Incarnation

In many ways, looking at the doctrine of Incarnation is looking at
Creation again from another vantage point. Creation is Incarnation.
That seems to be how humanity has come to faith, which is the

underside of the revelation of an accessible God. God is found
expressed and enfleshed in creation. Very early on in the dawn of
consciousness, it seems that humanity intuited the more in everything by asking the origin and ground of everything.

> The symbolic story of the beginning which speaks to us from
> the mythology of all ages is the attempt made by man's child-
> like prescientific consciousness to master problems and enigmas
> which are mostly beyond the grasp of even our developed modern
> consciousness. If our consciousness with epistemological resigna-
> tion is constrained to regard the question of the beginning as
> unanswerable and therefore unscientific, it may be right; but the
> psyche, which can neither be taught nor led astray by the self-
> criticism of the conscious mind, always poses the question afresh
> as one that is essential to it. . . . The original question about the
> origin of the world is at the same time the question of the origin
> of man, the origin of consciousness and the ego: it is the fateful
> question "Where did I come from?" that faces every human being
> as soon as he arrives upon the threshold of self-consciousness.[22]

For primitive humanity, the answers to these questions were
symbolized in the processes of nature, yet never simply contained
there. These myths always combined elements from nature in such
a way as to express a transcendence of nature. Preconscious humanity dwelt in immediacy with nature and in awe of it. One was not
able to distinguish nature from oneself; no difference between sub-
ject and object had yet emerged. Consequently, there was no real
distinguishing between external reality and one's own subjective
understanding. Nature was mimed as a way of affecting nature and
oneself. Nature was venerated. It was numinous in itself. It appeared
as the sacred reality determining one's destiny. Humanity saw nature
as the incarnation of the gods. The earth and the heavens came
forth from the bodies of the gods. Creation was Incarnation, and
thus fearsome and terrible as well as protective and generative.
The gradual spiritualization of the answer to the "whence question"
became more and more highly developed.

In their history, the Hebrews were able to move to their god
as the greatest among all others. Eventually they moved to seeing
Yahweh as the One God, Lord of Heaven and Earth. God spoke and
the heavens and earth were created. God spoke and they were created: male and female, in God's image. They came forth from  God's

word, God's breath. God made himself to live enfleshed in humanity. Predating the time when the Creation accounts were conceived, the Hebrews had a need to move this God out and beyond nature and humanity. The perceptions of animism and immanence give way to transcendence. At the same time the immanence answers are still there within consciousness because the experience, however crudely preserved, was a true human experience.

In the history of Israel, there grew up in many different strands an expectation of "one who is to come." "From the womb God has named this chosen one, indeed from the beginning of creation."[23] There is an expectation of one called the Son of Man.

> With the introduction of the son of man figure, a new name for God is brought in as well; a grey beard or one advanced in years (an ancient of days) see also Daniel 7:9. . . . Along with the very aged one appears someone else whose form looks like that of a man.[24]

Essential to all this was the oriental idea that everything earthly preexisted in heaven. Everything is prepared, especially everything that has to do with eschatological salvation from the creation of the world. Later on this "son of man" tradition became attached to the Davidic messiah tradition, and each one colors the other.

It is in a climate where such traditions live side by side with many other similar traditions that there comes on the scene in Galilee and Jerusalem a man from Nazareth named Jesus. About this Jesus, especially after his death, these deep-seated expectation traditions swirled like a whirlwind. They settled on him within a short time as people attempted to interpret the experience they had of him. The later versions of these traditions and their flowering in their association with Jesus are recorded in the gospel of John. This Gospel records that Jesus said, "Anyone who sees me, sees the Father."[25] That particular interpretation of the experience of Jesus rang so true to so many that it eventually secured this identity of Jesus with God in the religious faith of most of Western culture. By the church council of Nicea in the fourth century and Chalcedon in the fifth, the myth of the God-Man had found expression in Greco-Roman concepts and language as the doctrine of Incarnation.

Yet a religious utterance can only have such universal significance if it can be sensibly verified to a degree. "There must have been something in the historical situation to indicate that anyone who sees Jesus sees the Father."[26] This is true not only for those who personally experienced Jesus while he lived; somehow, this experience still must have been available in the fifth and fifteenth centuries and must still be a possibility today for such a doctrine to live on.

Such an experience can only be located in the possibility of experiencing the God revealed in Jesus. It is in the believer's own affirmation of the universal love of God that Jesus incarnated. Affirming that love personally opens one to something true to one's humanity, which can be pointed to at every stage of life, especially at life's crisis moments. To touch these dimensions and to allow them to illumine the mid-life transition, we do not start by

> saying that Jesus is God, the word of the eternal God made flesh, existing with the Father from eternity. Nor do we begin by speaking of the hypostatic union of the divine and human nature in the one person of the divine Logos.[27]

We need to begin with the experience that led to these mythological definitions of the experience. We need to begin with the experience of the first people who came to know Jesus as the exegete of God. For this we need to keep firmly in mind that Christianity is an historical religion and that real people experienced Jesus and spoke of the experience. We need to realize that it was in his own human history that Jesus experienced his own amazing relationship with God and that the consequences of that are his words and behavior.

The quest for that historical Jesus in this century with its new historical methods and hard and software has been fruitful even after it came up against the illusionary stone wall of the realization that we can't get at the exact words and deeds of Jesus. These questers showed us that Jesus had been handed on to us in the New Testament by a believing community, undoubtedly biased witnesses who gave us stories from his life as they remembered them from the vantage point of their post-Resurrection community experience. At that point at this "stone wall" Rudolf Bultmann, a giant of a New Testament scholar, declared that this was not a dead end because the faith of the Christian should in no way find itself dependent on the labors of historians.

> However, the perception of the man on the street . . . will notice

that the skepticism which seemed to accompany the historical
quest was and is equaled only by the persistent interest shown
in it. The old quest of the historical Jesus was followed by a new
quest—for all Bultmann could say or do.[28]

With this new quest there have been all kinds of attempts to discern
the consistent personality behind all the varying portraits of the man
Jesus. There have been attempts to see in the movement he started a
reflection of what Jesus himself said and did. Jesus certainly triggered
some extreme reactions. What kind of a man was this who was so
offensive as to be executed as a criminal by a large faction while being
the point of reference by which others began to define the ultimate
meaning and purpose of their lives? In the New Testament the primitive Church reflects or mirrors the Jesus event in its effects on a group
of people. Jesus himself is the rock-bottom center and source of the
unity of those effects. At the same time this Jesus was undoubtedly a
new experience of God for those who believed. That experience is
available even today for it is an incarnate experience, and the meeting
place for us, as it was for them, is our own humanity.

What was there in Jesus' manner of being human, in his manner
of life, that eventually drew people to the realization that they had
seen the human face of God? First, there was "Jesus' wonderful
freedom to do good."[29] Behind the Gospel accounts, one detects
a person who was very busy being good to all kinds of deprived
people. He seems to be crowded constantly by people seeking his
healing ministry whether that was physical, psychic or social healing. Compassion and graciousness mark his generous personal services. Nothing seems to thwart his doing good except exhaustion.
Certainly he was not thwarted by legalist criticism. He looks around
with anger at those who complain about his healing a man with
a withered hand in a synagogue on a Sabbath.[30] This must be a
recollection of many angry encounters with narrow interpretations
of the law, which he loved and said he came to fulfill.

This miracle tradition must have some basis in people's experience of Jesus. He certainly performed even more extraordinary
psychosocial miracles in calling and empowering people to live up
to their best selves and his vision of them. The Zacchaeus story[31] of
the thief who vowed to give back four times what he had stolen from
anyone is a recollection of this association with and transformation

of tax collectors. Levi,[32] who followed him, is another. There is also
the account of his having his feet washed by a prostitute whose great
love he praises.[33] The transformation wrought in and around this
woman and the woman taken in adultery[34] and the profound chord
of human solidarity in suffering that he touched then and touches
even today is hardly likely to have been invented. The story of the
woman taken in adultery whom he saves from stoning "is now a
floating piece of tradition precisely because it was both embar-
rassing and 'too like Jesus' to have been forgotten or invented."[35]

The authority of Jesus, too, was and still is an incredible experience. He did not teach like the ordinary Jewish rabbi with constant
reference to precedent. He speaks a wisdom that was and is awesome in its humanization. It stands on its own. His authority and
authorship is recognized in the repeated phrase "you have heard
but *I* say to you."[36] The shock of his questioning the absoluteness of
dietary laws is another example of his authority. He proclaims that
it is not what goes into a person's mouth, but what comes out of it
that defiles. He defends his disciples picking and eating grain on the
Sabbath. "From that time on they were afraid to ask him any more
questions."[37] This surely shows up the fearsomeness of Jesus' authority. His parables were filled with the same uncanny perception and
judgment. There is something incontestable even today in his
choices of the most profoundly human response.

Of all the audacious things Jesus said and did, surely the most
dumbfounding was his calling God, "Abba," the familiar form of
the word "father," and inviting everyone else to do the same. That
experience of God (in a believing Jew of the first century) from
which this name emanated is one of the most significant things that
compel people toward or away from Jesus, then and now. The God
of Jesus was not only personal, but intimate. He was not only transcendent, but immanent. The place of that meeting was within. It
certainly was within Jesus. Jesus reveals a Father who is utterly available and whose interest coincides at every point with the good of
each of his own. The Father, as Jesus talks about him, is always
there, just as the Prodigal's father was with him in the pig sty. It is
the certainty of that welcoming presence that moves the boy to get
up and return. Like leaven in dough, the Kingdom of God was
within. Each person could experience Abba and his Kingdom coming within as Jesus did.

It seems that after he was killed for this kind of audacity, the shattered, faithless followers were drawn back together by precisely such an experience of presence within. The Easter experience for each culminated in an inner power, wisdom and love that they named the Spirit of Christ. It was that Spirit that cried out in their hearts, "Abba." The God and his Kingdom that Jesus preached was surely both transcendent and immanent.

There was a whole new emphasis on each individual's experience of Abba, and yet there was a resultant communal experience. The greatest polarities of all live in the tension of the Jesus event. Each individual becomes free and responsible to author his or her own actions out of a love that dwells within. He or she can go beyond laws to Spirit. At the same time, this individuality with its source in God is the claim of every neighbor. Every human being thus has a claim on my love.

When they came back together after the Easter experience, together they advanced the Kingdom as a community. Jesus preached the Kingdom of God. They preached Jesus. As Jesus incarnated God and his Kingdom, they strove to incarnate Jesus. They saw themselves as members of God's body. Each had a uniqueness to bring to the whole. They were able to be both individual and community.

At the mid-life transition, individuation and inwardness come to the fore as matters of life and death. Incarnation is a way of interpreting and focusing both movements. In this time of transition, coming in touch again with the source of the authority of Jesus, his own uniqueness as Son, Word, and Image of God, is a way to be comfortable with one's own authority. If one can securely stand in one's own loneliness as different from everyone else, precisely as a unique daughter or son and word and image of God, one has a transpersonal footing. How much easier one can feel with what Jung calls the emergence of the Number Two Personality as it awakens at this time! That Self, seen as the image of God, supported the ego development in the first half of life. Now the ego moves out of center to make place for the Self. How much more easily can the ego befriend the unconscious elements if they are seen as parts of the true, unique Self that is to become an incarnation of God.

One can seize one's own authority without needing to put others down, without a sense of competition, if individuation has this kind of meaning. This kind of true individuation gradually moves into bearing the tension of the individual-community polarity in a truly loving way. The Self can be truly loved and freed of accommodating effacement. Generativity can become a way of expressing and incarnating the Self.

In experiencing one's own individuation, one has names to give it from the Christian myth of Incarnation and this has the reciprocal effect of furthering the individuating.

Going inward to discover the universe within oneself is more possible if one has had an Abba Amma experience. One finds one's whole being expanded in a faith experience of being ultimately loved. Trust in the ultimate benevolence of life and the outer universe flows from this. Openness to life and the future becomes eternal possibility. One is invited to find the Kingdom within oneself. As one in the second half of life spends more time getting in touch with the inner self, one can be less afraid, knowing oneself forgiven by a loving God. The inner journey is made with a protecting God who goes before to show the way. With trust in inner wisdom, power, and Love, it is easier to begin to make the inside and outside more alike. It is the task of the transition to begin to make one's Self with new meanings, values, and goals incarnate. One brings out the treasures from within the Self and makes them visible in one's life-style. One is more secure in letting those treasures be seen if one trusts the Self. Christ suffered death rather than be untrue to his own awareness of Self. Wanting like him to be true to the real Self in all one says and does ensures that even mistakes and sin can be undone in an ever-possible Easter transformation. In the Christian myth of Incarnation, no suffering is ever lost. Christ, in solidarity with humanity, had to suffer all these things so as to enter into his glory. The evil he endured never separated him from God's love, no matter what the outer appearances. If unconditional love cannot be earned, neither can it be lost. It can only be rejected.

The Christian doctrine of Incarnation lights up the terrain of one's inner world with the unconditional love of God. Such love accepted again and again in the depth of oneself cannot help but overflow in love of Self and others and in outer life that moves in a healthy direction for oneself and the world. In this way one not only verifies the myth of the Incarnation, but one becomes oneself a continuation of that Incarnation ongoing in history until the eschaton.

### Notes

1. Isa. 64:7.

2. Jer. 18:1-6.

3. Guy P. Couturier, "Jeremiah," in *The Jerome Biblical Commentary*, ed. Raymond E. Brown et al. (Englewood Cliffs, N.J.: Prentice-Hall, 1968), p. 317.

4. Jurgen Moltmann, *The Future of Creation* (Philadelphia: Fortress Press, 1979), p. 116.

5. *Ibid.*, p. 117.

6. Gerhard Van Rad, *Old Testament Theology*, trans. D. M. G. Stalker (New York: Harper and Row, 1962), p. 138.

7. Ibid., p. 138.

8. Moltmann, *The Future of Creation*, p. 118.

9. 1 Cor. 15:28.

10. Moltmann, *The Future of Creation*, p. 119.

11. Rev. 21:1.

12. Rev. 22:5.

13. Rom. 8:18-24.

14. William M. Thompson, *Christ and Consciousness* (New York: Paulist Press, 1977), p. 53.

15. *Ibid.*, p. 10.

16. Ira Progoff, *The Well and the Cathedral* (New York: Dialogue House, 1977), p. 147.

17. James P. Mackey, *Jesus, the Man and Myth* (New York: Paulist Press, 1979), p. 78.

18. Edward Edinger, "Depth Psychology as the New Dispensation: Reflections on Jung's *Answer to Job*," in *Quadrant*, Winter 1979, p. 8.

19. Edward Schillebeeckx, *Jesus: An Experiment in Christology*, trans. Hubert Hoskins (New York: Seabury Press, 1979), p. 628.

20. Rom. 8:35-39.

21. Thess. 4:13.

22. Erich Neumann, *The Origins and History of Consciousness*, trans. R. F. C. Hull, Bollingen Series, no. 42 (Princeton: Princeton University Press, 1970), p. 7.

23. En. 48:3.

24. Schillebeeckx, *Jesus: An Experiment in Christology*, p. 462.

25. John 14:9.

26. Schillebeeckx, *Jesus: An Experiment in Christology*, p. 603.

27. Karl Rahner and Wilhelm Thusing, *A New Chistology*, trans. David Smith and Verdent Green (New York: Seabury Press, 1980), p. 4.

28. Mackey, *Jesus the Man and Myth*, p. 4.

29. Schillebeeckx, *Jesus: An Experiment in Christology*, p. 183.

30. Mark 3.

31. Luke 19:1-10.

32. Luke 5:27-30.

33. Luke 7:36-38.

34. John 8:1-11.

35. John A. T. Robinson, *The Human Face of God* (Philadelphia: Westminster Press, 1973), p. 98.

36. Matt. 5.

37. Luke 20:40.

# 5

# A Mid-life Task: Clarifying and Owning One's Values

And so for the first time in my life perhaps (although I am supposed to meditate every day!), I took the lamps and, leaving the zone of everyday occupations and relationships where everything seems clear, I went down into my inmost self, to the deep abyss whence I feel dimly that my power of action emanates. But as I moved further and further away from the conventional certainties by which social life is superficially illuminated, I became aware that I was losing contact with myself. At each step of the descent a new person was disclosed within me of whose name I was no longer sure, and who no longer obeyed me. And when I had to stop my exploration because the path faded from beneath my steps, I found a bottomless abyss at my feet, and out of it came—arising I know not from where—the current which I dare to call my life.[1]

In these words, paleontologist Teilhard de Chardin shared with us his moment of the discovery of the unconscious, the Self, the current of his life. We are each called to that moment. It is the invitation of the afternoon of life and comprises the glorious tasks of the second half of life. It is the call to wholeness, the call to go beyond what we know of ourselves and to gradually encounter all the myriad aspects of ourselves, to discover the depths of who we are, and to integrate the polarities and contradictions that are found within us and contribute to our vitality and uniqueness.

We spend the first half of life adapting to our outer environment. We surrender to the environment of the womb that creates us and we are formed by the climate of those significant others in our early life. Unconsciously we learn to win love, acceptance, and approval by being good, quiet, funny—whatever wins approval. After, the family, church, school, friends, and society in general enters into our formation. In the stage of childhood from the mother's womb to the transition of adolescence, our consciousness gradually develops. In early infancy I am one with the breast that feeds me but the day comes when I see mother as "other" and I verbalize the differentiation with a word that coins the new discovery "me." Now the world revolves around me and it is a long, painful lesson to discover that the world is filled with other "me's."

In adapting to this world we take on the values and goals that are outside of us, creating for ourselves a corresponding self-image. Even adolescence only gives us the time to break away from the psychic womb of parents to leap into the moral dictation and constraint of some self-chosen other authorities. The first half of life is spent finding authoritative answers to life's questions and decisions primarily outside of the self. What kind of work to pursue, what kind of people to befriend, how and to whom to commit ourselves, all this is dictated to us primarily by the environment that surrounds us—society and culture.

Brian Hall sees a person's life span succeeding in four stages of consciousness. Each stage has a progressive movement that incorporates a pair of primary values. At each stage of consciousness or growth we find our core meaning in the values of the stage. The four stages and growth in consciousness that Hall's theory demonstrates complement Carl Jung's four stages of life: childhood, youth, adulthood, and old age. For Hall, the distinction between the first two stages of consciousness and the later two is that in the first two, authority is external to the self and in the later two, because of the changes in consciousness, the person takes authority into him- or herself. This movement from external authority to internal authority occurs in a transition time which Hall calls "No-Man's-Land." Like Jung, who sees the transition from the first half of life to the second as the most traumatic and crucial, Hall, while recognizing the crisis of each transition, highlights the importance and significance of the move from Phase II to Phase III. ". . . When a person moves from one phase of consciousness to another there is a radical reorganization of the manner in which he [or she] chooses values and of criteria by which he [or she] makes these choices. Consequently the movement from one phase to another is often traumatic for an individual. The most traumatic experience comes when a person moves from Phase II to Phase III."[2]

TRANSITIONS IN CONSCIOUSNESS[3]

1. WORLD AS MYSTERY  
   Self as Center

   A. SELF-PRESERVATION  
   B. SELF-DELIGHT (PHYSICAL)

2. WORLD AS PROBLEM  
   Self as Belonging  
   NO-MAN'S-LAND

   A. SELF-WORTH  
   B. SELF-COMPETENCE (SOCIAL)  
   AMBIVALENT IN VALUE  
   PRIORITIES AND NEEDS

3. WORLD AS PROJECT  
   AND  
   INVENTION  
   Self as Independent

   A. INDEPENDENCE SELF  
   CHOSEN (CONSCIENCE)  
   B. BEING SELF  
   INTERDEPENDENT

4. WORLD AS MYSTERY  
   CARED FOR  
   Self as Life Given

"No-Man's-Land" is a good name for the transition time. We are neither here nor there, betwixt and between. "The person who is between any two stages sees the practicality and need for values out of both stages and as such can become tremendously ambivalent."[4]

The person in mid-life experiences an inner need and compulsion to go within. We want to discover our own inner resources, strengths, weaknesses, and potentials. Indeed, we want to discover who we really are. There is a gradual realization that we are not just the person we thought we were. There is more to each of us. This yearning for knowledge of and an encounter with the true Self comes to us in the disguise of restlessness, boredom, dreariness, depression. The strong, apparently self-determined and self-committed people of a decade or two ago no longer find meaning in the values, goals, or choices of yesterday. Yet we are ambiguous about all this. There are feelings of guilt, worthlessness, and failure. All of this is an invitation to go within, to begin the journey of self-discovery. The mid-life person is called to experience not only an expansion of consciousness regarding the outer environment but a growing consciousness of the Self within. The individuation process is the movement toward the harmonious complementarity of the conscious and unconscious aspects of oneself to form a totality that is the Self. The Self "embraces not only the conscious but also the unconscious psyche, and is therefore, so to speak, a personality which we also are."[5] "Basically, individuation consists of constantly renewed, constantly needed attempts to amalgamate the inner images with outer experience. . . . In successful moments a part of the self is actualized as a union of inside and outside. Then a man [or woman] can repose in [him- or herself], become self-fulfilled, and an aura of authenticity emanates from him."[6]

As this journey in self-discovery begins, we are called to dethrone the gods of our youth. "The gods we are called to dethrone are the idolized values of the conscious world."[7] John Shea believes that the experience of disenchantment initiates us into a mature religious consciousness. "At first the experience of disenchantment appears negative. It is resented and seen as destructive of personal convictions and purposes. What was thought to be the case has proved otherwise. This is not merely the pain of being wrong or the pain of loss but the pain of being deceived."[8] But this shaking of the foundations, this engagement in "the process of disenchantment is also a process of disengagement, a double freeing."[9] This very disenchantment frees us from the tyrannical control and constriction of the ego and launches us on a search for our own true, genuine values and goals. Gradually we discover our own true values in the process of living life and becoming attuned to our own inner selves. Never again will we accept a ready-made map for our life's journey and adventure. Like Teilhard, we are invited to "take the lamp and go within," contacting and relating to the myriad aspects of the Self and drawing from the inner spring of life as we enter into the genuine movement and current of each Self.

Levinson also speaks of something similar to Hall's "No-Man's-Land." He calls this sensation being "on the boundary." "During the mid-life transition itself, however, the person is truly 'on the boundary': . . . both in early adulthood and in middle adulthood. This transition separates the two eras, enabling one to end so that the next can begin. It serves also to connect them, bringing about interchange so that the past can be drawn upon and used selectively in building for the future."[10] The transition period is the result of both disenchantment and disillusionment. But both are angels in disguise because they force us to enter the search for our own Selves and for our own values. This movement toward the true Self constitutes the major conversion of life. It is the crucial turning point in our process of becoming human. Not everyone accepts this challenge. Some refuse the journey inward. They return to their old ways, close off consciousness, foreclose the future, and remain entrenched in the first half of life. Still others refuse the long, slow process of integration. They discard the identity of the first half of life and all its values. "The snag about a radical conversion into one's opposite is that one's former life suffers repression and thus produces just as unbalanced a state as existed before, when the counterparts of the conscious virtues and values were still repressed and unconscious."[11]

To be human is to be called to be a mystic, and the first half of life prepares us for this most human of adventures. ". . . Mysticism or contemplation is a return to harmonious union: it is a process of reconciliation, of inner unification, of magnificent justification. . . . That is to say, it makes us one with ourselves, one with the human race, one with the All which is God."[12] The underlying myth that drove Jung on was the call to the exploration of the psyche. He believed that modern man was sick because he had ignored and disowned his unconscious life. The conscious (ego) and the unconscious (self) were split. Only genuine mysticism could heal the split and bring about a reconciliation. The greatest hindrance to the individuation process is materialism, the opposite of mysticism. "The hypothesis of an unconscious underlying consciousness is the hallmark of psychological research in this century. Almost simultaneously, the natural sciences framed the corresponding hypothesis of a hidden ability underlying the phenomenal world."[13] Nevertheless, despite this new consciousness, the majority of people are still entrenched in a materialistic attitude, not a mystical one.

The materialistic person values only consciousness and ignores, despises, or denies unconsciousness, which the mystic learns to embrace as his or her other half. The materialist hooks on to the familiar and evades the unfamiliar, which the mystic can befriend. The materialist sees himself as good and projects his shadow on others while the mystic comes to love his shadow and see within it. The materialist avoids all internal conflict and paradox while the mystic lives with the questions and accepts the asceticism of conflict, believing it will lead to good. The materialist separates from her true Self and others while the mystic seeks to encounter the true Self and the inner reality that connects him or her to each other person. The materialist is entrenched in one viewpoint, unable to accept ambiguity, while the mystic can embrace the contradiction of the polarities of the opposites and await their transformation. The materialist slavishly grasps onto the values and goals of youth while the mystic enters into the relativity of all the chosen ideals, values, and goals. The materialist is rationalistic, ignoring the full Self, intuition, and the life of the Spirit while the mystic draws life from the heart and the Spirit within. The materialist speaks literally and decisively while the mystic communicates in myths and symbols. Harvey Cox tells us that in sleep the materialist becomes his truly human Self, pointing to the proper nature that is not being lived out. "However unreligious or 'secularized' someone may claim to be, he instantly relapses into being a mythic and symbolic creature as soon as he falls asleep and begins to dream."[14]

The transition from the first half of life to the second half demands of us a conversion from materialism to mysticism. Indeed this is the mid-life crisis: Will I make the conversion, will I begin to see with my inner eye and thus move toward wholeness? The first half of life requires more of a materialistic style to deal with the adaptation to the outer world and the development of the ego. In a move toward integration and wholeness, we must gradually adapt to our inner world and the development of the true Self. This requires a mystical attitude and stance toward the Self and life. Ira Progoff writes of the obstacle to this conversion, materialism:

> Modern culture is predominantly outer oriented. Its dominant values are personal competitiveness, conspicuous consumption, status climbing, and the like. More important, and related to this, is the fact that the primary terms for its perception of reality are sensory and materialistic. . . . They are materialistic in the more specific sense of the attitude that is adapted in valuing and judging life experiences. In this outlook, the dynamics of the outer

world are felt to be of much greater importance than the dynamics of the inner world, which are often dismissed as vague, fuzzy, and rather unreal. This particular form of materialism, which is the attitude that rejects the reality of the inward, sets the terms in which individuals experience and enact their lives in much of modern culture.[15]

The conversion of mid-life demands that the inner world become as real to us as the outer world. The second half of life is a journey inward and it is from our own inner experience that we slowly learn to discern our own genuine values. For Jung and for Teilhard, the encounter with the mystery within was an encounter with the mystery of God. The person on the "inward journey" is in search of the will of God for him or her, and that is to be in search of the authentic inward movement of his or her life.

If mysticism is integral to our humanity, so too is owning our values and making choices. This is how we become a Self. In the second half of life our values and choices must flow from our inner life. Authenticity is needed in the second half of life. We are driven to discover our values not materialistically, but mystically. Our own welfare and the welfare of the universe is dependent upon our growing centeredness and authenticity.

For some people, "centeredness" comes naturally at this time; for others, it is something that must at first be actively and consciously engaged in. We spend most of our daily life as extroverts. "We are constantly attracted, distracted, dispersed by countless sensations, impressions, preoccupations, memories of the past, projects for the future; we are everywhere except in our self-consciousness; in the consciousness of that which we are in reality."[16] One must learn to take the time and give Self the space to be disengaged from all the bustle of life and experience oneself as more than all of this. We equate ourselves with our egos, our bodies, emotions, desires, intellects, etc., and that identification is injurious to the inward journey and to growth. On one hand, I must know how I feel about this and that. I must grow more and more in touch with my own bodily movements and emotions. On the other hand, I must be able to disengage myself from them and know experientially that I am more than them.

"What am I then? What remains after discarding from my self-identity the physical, emotional and mental contents of my per-

sonality, of my ego? It is the essence of myself — a center of pure
self-consciousness and self-realization. It is the permanent factor
in the ever varying flow of my personal life. . . . I am a center of
awareness and of power."[17]

It is crucial that we experience our center, for all our value judgments and decisions must eventually flow from this center. In "No-
Man's-Land," and "on the boundary" we experience a disintegra-
tion and a fragmentation that accompanies our disenchantment,
and a corresponding loss of values and goals. It is imperative that
we experience ourself as more than this. Centeredness is a unifying
experience that allows us to experience unity and oneness despite
the fragmentation. It allows us to distance ourselves from the problem at hand, to experience the "Self," the inner core, and gradually
to move toward a new and different self-possession and wholeness.

*Les Miserables* by Victor Hugo is a splendid story of humanization, transformation, and self-transcendence. The hero of Hugo's
story, Jean Valjean, was the sole support of his widowed sister and
her seven children. One winter evening, in desperation, he stole
bread from a neighbor's home to save the starving children. In
turn, Valjean was sent to prison for five years. He tried to escape
four times; as a result, he spent a total of nineteen years in prison
for breaking a window and stealing a loaf of bread. Valjean suc-
ceeded in disguising his identity and built a new and prosperous life
for himself while growing more human and mystical in the grace of
a new birth. His identity was ultimately discovered and he was
again thrown into jail.

Hugo presents a marvelous scene where Valjean escapes and
returns to his home, where he is Mayor. The police pursue him. He
is giving instructions about his belongings to Sister Sulpice as the
police arrive on the chase. The portress tells the pursuers, "My good
sir, I swear to you in the name of God, that nobody has come in
here the whole day . . ."[18] Pushing past her, the police enter the
room where Sister Sulpice has been kneeling as if in prayer. She has
never lied in her life and honesty and truthfulness are part of her
ego and identity. "Sister," the police question, "are you alone in this
room?" "Yes." "Jean Valjean — you have not seen him?" "No," she
answers.[19]

The lies did not unmake her; rather, they allowed her to make
the leap from outer authority to inner authority. They blast open in

one quick stroke the failure of the law at times to do good. They allowed her to crash the idol of "truthfulness," not make a god of it. The triumph of the moment is felt as we laugh at Valjean's parting words to the nun: "May this falsehood be remembered to thee in Paradise."[20]

And so it is. Truthfulness is an objective good to be valued and upheld but never to be made into a god. Having grown up with truthfulness, one reaches the point of internalizing the virtue and therefore owning it, not being owned by it.

It is a superficial example of the crossing of the boundary from external authority to internal authority, but nonetheless real. On the more serious side, listen to the words of Paulo Freire. Here he is speaking of our changing times, the expansion of consciousness regarding the masses, but this is comparable to the movement of an individual from the first half of life to the second. These same words apply to the person in mid-life transition.

> . . . A society beginning to move from one epoch to another requires the development of an especially flexible, critical spirit. Lacking such a spirit, men cannot perceive the marked contradictions which occur in society as emerging values in search of affirmation and fulfillment clash with earlier values seeking self-preservation. The time of epochal transition constitutes an historical–cultural "tidal wave." Contradictions increase between the ways of being, understanding, behaving and valuing which announce the future. As the contradictions deepen, the "tidal wave" becomes stronger and its climate increasingly emotional. This shock between a yesterday which is losing relevance but still seeking to survive, and a tomorrow which is gaining substance, characterize the phase of transition as a time of announcement and a time of decision. Only, however, to the degree that the choices result from a critical perception of the contradiction are they real and capable of being transformed in action. Choice is illusory to the degree it represents the expectations of others.[21]

Christiaan Barnard, the 56-year-old doctor who performed the first human heart transplant in 1968, speaks of his changing goals in an interview.

> It's true that the only advantage of getting to the top of the mountain is to see the next mountain to climb. But it's more than that. You also need the strength and drive and enthusiasm to climb the

next peak. I've lost a lot of that. I've lost it because there are not many more peaks in medicine to climb. We have achieved so much in cardiac surgery. The other thing is, with getting older, you don't have that drive, you don't need that tremendous feeding of the ego anymore. So my ambition now in life is to enjoy what time I have left. To enjoy it in different ways. My career as a doctor has mostly ended.[22]

There is a genuine asceticism requested of us in living life with zest and entering into certain tasks wholeheartedly, knowing that it is only for a time. There are tasks and goals in life that call for a selfless commitment, that demand that we give ourselves "a free gift with no strings attached." If you meet the challenge, you and the world are the richer. Parenting is an example of this. Children step into our lives in a most unique way and only for a time. They are not really ours. They are a gift to the universe. We help to give that gift by parenting and letting go. Martin Marty speaks of this when he reflects on parents and friendship.

> Parents who make exhausting demands for the affection of their children have not learned that a family is not exclusive or per-manent. A couple comes on stage; they are to reveal the family as an art form. It is not an art like architecture or painting, finished and there for ages. Their art is like the ballet, to be danced when the curtain goes up and the stage lights on. Soon the footlights will dim, the house lights will go up, the curtain will fall. The dance is over and the dancers move on, with memories, snapshots, and other stages ahead. Parents who do not learn how to let go are doing a disservice to family relations. But if parents and children are friends, they will have been learning how to bid good-byes.[23]

But not all enter into this natural asceticism. The loss of children, the "empty nest," leaves some holding on resolutely. They psychologically and spiritually strangle the very ones they gave birth to in numerous and devious ways. One wonders if the Scriptures do not reflect this human problem as a warning and reminder to parents as much as to children. "This at last is bone from my bones, and flesh from my flesh! This is to be called woman, for this was taken from man. This is why a man leaves his father and mother and joins himself to his wife, and they become one body."[24] Many parents cling to the task not long theirs because they refuse to let go and enter into the asceticism of the moment, which can create for them the solitariness necessary to awaken within themselves other aspects of Self. This would be the key to new goals, new vitality, and new and vital ways of continuing mature and nurturing relationships of a new style with children and grandchildren.

> This is what makes the transition . . . so terribly difficult and bitter for many people . . . . They cling to the illusion of youth or to their children . . . . One sees it especially in mothers, who find their sole meaning in their children and imagine they will sink into a bottomless void when they give them up . . . . But the problems that crop up at this age are no longer to be solved by the old recipes: the hand of this clock cannot be put back. What youth found and must find outside, the man of life's afternoon must find within himself.[25]

The owning of one's own values calls the mid-life person to a process of internalizing authority; that is, coming to discover the authority within the Self. Owning one's values calls the person to the acceptance of growth and change. This occurs in the letting go of values, tasks, and goals no longer compatible to our real situation and turning inward to discover the true meaning of life.

The mid-life person is called to be engaged in an adventure of self-awareness and self-knowledge that will lead to integration and wholeness. It is not an adventure in selfishness. It is the human task, the moral journey, a coming to oneself, in the greatest contribution that can be made to this agonizing world of ours, trembling for wholeness: a new birth.

> Self-discovery or rediscovery, self-conquest or reconquest, moving from habit to the creation of a new self, taking on rather than submitting, mastering a situation which previously controlled us, are the essential steps toward conversion. Conversion is the desire to become "more" than we already are. It is being faithful to oneself. Becoming aware of "who I am" in order to become "who I should." And if conversion involves breaking away, this is breaking from all the forms of alienation, even the subtlest ones, that up till then had prevented me from becoming myself.[26]

Many people in mid-life transition are taking their first steps, some just crawling, in the experience of coming to know their own feelings and emotions. The tasks of the first half of life were so demanding, and the ego development so constricting, that the unconscious repression and suppression of feelings and emotions make whole other aspects of Self strangers to us. This was Teilhard's experience, too. "At each step of the descent a new person was disclosed within me of whose name I was no longer sure, and who no longer obeyed me."[27] It is necessary that we give ourselves the time and leisure for this pursuit of self-knowledge and growth. Is this not what Jesus did in the forty days he spent in the desert? Aren't the temptations the witness to the struggle for balance and integration that flowed from a new consciousness and a genuine coming to oneself? Is not this self-knowledge, this encounter with the shadow, with evil, the core reason why Jesus could say, "Woman, where are they? Has no one condemned you?" "No one, sir." "Neither do I condemn you," [28] And again, why else could Jesus so enter into the experience of Peter's threefold denial that he could search out the perfect cure, thus reflecting his ability to "walk in Peter's shoes," which only an integrated, whole person could do? Witness the balm, the healing of the trinitarian words, "Simon, Son of John, do you love Me?"[29]

Coming to terms with our own shadow and all the irrational, suppressed, repressed aspects of our human personalities is essential in the process toward integration and wholeness. In the first half of life we developed a "goodness" required by society and eventually, even more authoritatively, by ourselves. That "goodness" was dictated to us by outside standards and outside standards, eventually internalized, were in fact necessary for us in order to adapt to society and achieve a plan for ourselves in the world. Now in the mid-life movement toward authenticity, freedom, and creativity, our personality demands that we own the despised and rejected aspects of ourselves and in that owning touch the powers of re-creation that are within them. "Love yourself" does not refer to parts of ourselves but to the totality of Self. We cannot surrender to our shadow or to the irrational aspects of our psyche, but we must negotiate with them. It is within the forces of our own nature that we find the sources of creativity and liberation. The demonic rule of our "ego" and our "goodness" leads to an imbalanced, puritanical, false goodness and pharisaical blindness — the source of all personal and social evil.

The temptations of Jesus were an experience of the fullness of humanity, which includes irrationality. The self-transcendence that Jesus gave witness to was also an understanding of human nature and all its possibilities for good and for evil that made him able to call for not separating the chaff from the wheat. Perhaps the institutional church has always had a difficulty in presenting the Jesus who was inclusive and who went contrary to established norms. The churches can be guilty of what Harvey Cox calls "The seduction of the spirit." "The seduction of the spirit, in short, is the calculated twisting of people's natural and healthy religious instincts for purposes of control and domination. It is the cruelest abuse of religion because it slyly enlists people in their own manipulation."[30] The Hebrew Scriptures are filled with deeply spiritual people who in no way fit our norms: Moses the murderer, David the adulterer, Jacob the deceiver, Abraham, who deserts his father. Erich Neumann brings our attention to this. "In classical Judaism, the man of God was by no means necessarily distinguished by the high level of his ethical conduct. The relationship between the divine and the world in which man was actually incorporated was originally brought about by listening to the inner voice of the divine in man, not by the performance of prescribed ethical duties."[31]

Throughout Christian history beginning with Jesus, we have had rare individuals who tend to blast open the narrow, preconceived, constricting concept of the mature adult personality. The world reacted in shock, horror, delight, perplexity, and wonder, when a *Life* Magazine cover showed Pope John XXIII decked in the regalia of cardinal, cocktail glass in one hand, cigarette in another, and the bulging red that showed a good appetite. Yet this apparent lack of asceticism (of one kind) enveloped a man in the world who turned the Catholic Church around (conversion). He left the Vatican to visit prisons, and had the awareness and fortitude to comment on the stale air within his church. It was John who broke through the polarities of: Church-world, Roman Catholic-non-Catholic, prayer-work, believer-nonbeliever, Christian-Jew, heaven-earth. It was John who saw through the pharisaical uprightness of the Roman Catholic community and led it into a council that admitted its rightful share in the breakup of Christianity in the Protestant Reform. In that council, the Roman Catholic community moved from being exclusive to being inclusive. This changing world view of Catholicism, this growth of consciousness, has placed the Catholic Church today "on the boundary line," in "No-Man's-Land," betwixt and between. A new consciousness ushers in the crumbling of long-held values, goals, positions. The living experience that ushered in the new consciousness ushers in a process that gradually leads to new values and goals sometimes the exact opposite of those previously held, while maintaining the balance of an integration and an openness to the positive in the previously held value. Jung wrote of this with regard to personal growth, but in this instance it is perhaps comparable to the process of the Church becoming:

> "The transition from the morning to afternoon means a revalua- tion of the earlier values. There comes the urgent need to ap- preciate the value of the opposite of our former ideals, to perceive the error in our former convictions, to recognize the untruth in our former truth, and to feel how much antagonism and even hatred lay at what, until now, had passed for love."[32]

It is the spirit within us, found in the core of our own Selves, that slowly and painfully weaves its way through anxiety, confusion, ten- sion, and conflict to hear the rhythm of our own personal tune made up of choices and values that are truly our own. This becomes our great contribution to the world. The authenticity of one person enhances the coming authenticity of the world.

Jesus broke through the collective values of Jewish society in response to the inner insights and the growing awareness that he ex- perienced. John XXIII broke through the collective values of four hundred years of the Roman Catholic community voicing the inner insights and growing awareness of his experience. "The courage to make an individual appraisal of values which declares its in- dependence of the values of the collective in matters of good and evil is one of the most difficult demands made on the individual by the new ethic."[33]

We must attune ourselves to the voice within. We must continue in the process of growth, in obedience to that growing awareness.

> To surrender the moral certainty about good and evil provided by the old ethic, stamped as it was with the approval of the collective, and to accept the ambiguity of the inner experience is always a difficult undertaking for the individual, since in every case it in- volves a venture with the unknown, with all the dangers which the acceptance of evil brings with it for every responsible ego."[34]

This is the new asceticism. It is the asceticism of the second half of life. It prepares us to come to personal choices and values that flow from our interior and genuinely reflect our experience of living and relating in this world, our environment within and without. This authenticity and individuality is to be the leaven of the world. All this takes time. Our own psychic changes progress slowly, but then are lasting. Quick conversions and fits of idealism usually lose their effect. The transformation of the culture is even slower and takes a century or more.

This call to authenticity and wholeness is a call to justice. Tradition has called Joseph, the spouse of Mary, the "Just Man." He responds in the Christian story to Mary's pregnancy not rationally but intuitively and mystically. He did not use the law to guide his response, to make his decision "correct," or to wipe out ambiguity and give him the certitude of moral uprightness. He responded instead from the core of his being. Joseph was a "just man." "The just man is following his deepest spiritual instincts which tell him of the promptings of the Holy Spirit. He is beyond the law."[35]

Mid-life is an invitation to "justice." Justice demands that the reasons for our being be discovered and lived out. Justice demands that attention and respect be given to our full personality in all its myriad aspects and possibilities. Justice demands that our authenticity make a contribution to the authenticity of the coming Kingdom. Justice demands that our unique gifts and creativity make their contribution to this world of ours. Justice demands that the first half of life surrender to the tasks of the second half of life. Justice demands that the inner voice be listened to. Justice demands that we deal with the pain of rebirth. Justice demands that we reach our full potential in awareness and consciousness. Justice demands that we have the fullness of healthy self-expression and its corresponding virtues: "spontaneity, genuineness, originality, freedom."[36]

> During the mid-life transition, a man needs to reduce his heavy involvement in the external world. To do the work of reappraisal and de-illusionment, he must turn inward. He has to discover what his turmoil is about, and when he hurts. He wants to find and lick his wounds. Having been overly engaged in his worldly struggles, he needs to become more engaged with himself. In this period the archetypal Self takes on greater definition and vitality. It becomes a more active internal figure, someone that the conscious ego must learn to talk with and listen to. The Self is the "I"

a man has in mind when he asks "What do I really want?" How do
I feel about my life?" He is feeling, in effect, that his present
relationships, goals, and style of living are in certain crucial
respects not right for the Self. He needs to separate himself from
the striving ego and the external pressures, so that he can better
hear the voice from within.[37]

This is the mid-life transition, moving toward clarifying and
owning one's value and one's values through growing awareness
within and without. Teilhard himself was deeply involved in the
within and without. "O God, that at all times you may find me as
you desire me and where you would have me be, that you may lay
hold on me fully, both by the Within and the Without of myself,
grant that I may never break this double thread of my life."[38]

## Notes

1. Pierre Teilhard de Chardin, *The Divine Milieu* (New York: Harper
and Row, 1960),pp. 76-77.

2. Brian Hall, *The Development of Consciousness* (New York: Paulist
Press, 1976), p. 105.

3. *Ibid.*, p. 56 and p. 106.

4. *Ibid.*, p. 166.

5. C. G. Jung, *Two Essays on Analytical Psychology*, trans. R. F. C.
Hull (New York: Meridian Books, 1956), p. 177.

6. Aniela Jaffe, *The Myth of Meaning*, trans. R. F. C. Hull (New York:
G. P. Putnam's Sons, 1971), p. 79.

7. C. G. Jung, *Modern Man in Search of a Soul*, trans. W. S. Dell and
Gary F. Baynes (New York: Harcourt, Brace and World, Inc., 1933), p.
212.

8. John Shea, *Stories of God* (Chicago: Thomas More Press, 1978), p.
35.

9. *Ibid.*, p. 36.

10. Daniel J. Levinson, *The Seasons of a Man's Life* (New York: Ballantine Books, 1978), p. 50.

11. C. G. Jung, *Two Essays on Analytical Psychology*, p. 75.

12. William Johnston, *The Inner Eye of Love*, p. 126.

13. Aniela Jaffe, *The Myth of Meaning*, p. 29.

14. Harvey Cox, *The Seduction of the Spirit* (New York: Simon and
Schuster, 1973), p. 13.

15. Ira Progoff, *The Symbolic and the Real* (New York: McGraw-Hill, 1963), p. 37.

16. Roberto Assagioli, *Psychosynthesis* (New York: Hobbs Dorman & Co., 1965), p. 118.

17. *Ibid.*, p. 119.

18. Victor Hugo, *Les Miserables* (New York: Dodd, Mead and Company, 1862), p. 106.

19. *Ibid.*, p. 107.

20. *Ibid.*

21. Paulo Freire, *Education for Critical Consciousness* (New York: Continuum Publishing Company, 1980), p. 7.

22. Christian Barnard, as interviewed by Dan Cryer in *Long Island* (*Newsday*'s Sunday Magazine, February 15, 1981), p. 46.

23. Martin E. Marty, *Friendship* (Allen, Texas: Argus Communications, 1980), pp. 172-73.

24. Gen. 2:23-24.

25. C. G. Jung, *Two Essays on Analytical Psychology*, pp. 74-75.

26. Jacques Leclercq, *This Day Is Ours*, trans. Dinah Livingstone (Maryknoll, New York: Orbis Books, 1980), p. 52.

27. Pierre Teilhard de Chardin, *The Divine Milieu*, p. 77.

28. John 8:10-11.

29. John 21:16.

30. Harvey Cox, *The Seduction of the Spirit*, p. 132.

31. Erich Neumann, *Depth Psychology and the New Ethic*, trans. Eugene Rolfe (New York: G. P. Putnam's Sons, 1969), p. 132.

32. C. G. Jung, *Two Essays on Analytical Psychology*, p. 75.

33. Erich Neumann, *Depth Psychology and a New Ethic*, p. 110.

34. *Ibid.*, p. 108.

35. William Johnston, *The Inner Eye of Love*, p. 125.

36. Rollo May, *The Art of Counseling* (Nashville: Abingdon, 1939), pp. 190-92.

37. Daniel J. Levinson, *The Seasons of a Man's Life*, p. 241.

38. Pierre Teilhard de Chardin, *The Divine Milieu*, p. 180.

# 6

## Storytelling:
## A Way of Dealing
## with Mid-life
## Crisis and Transition

### Having a Story

Each of us experiences life as a running narrative. The disparate particles of our experience hook themselves to one another to tell a story. Outer life tells a story. Inner life tells a story. When we look around we see stories all around us. All day long we listen to fragments of other's stories. The telephone, the television, films, and books bombard us with stories. We love well-told stories. Our own life pushes to tell its story well. We feel a sense of our success or failure in the telling of that story.

We are so close to this way of swimming in a river of a story that we scarcely notice it. Yet it is as essential to our human existence as air. "Not to have a story to live out is to experience nothingness; the primal formlessness of human life below the threshold of narrative structuring."[1] Ongoing story is the very structure in which we live. It is our way of ordering the chaos of each second's living. Memory and identity are utterly connected. We hold the narrative in the sanctuary of memory, or somewhere beneath memory where memory can reach at least some of it. Human life would be formless without this linking, this way of relating and relating *to* events.

Each of us needs to feel underpinned by that narrative. Jung discovered this in his work with his patients. "Each of us has a story, derangement comes when the story is denied or rejected. Rediscovery of the story is the cure."[2] Our very mental balance is tied up with keeping in touch with and holding fast to the narrative sequence that underlies our thoughts. If we do not, we will be forever losing our grip on the reality of our own identities with the passage of separate moments.

There seems to be a quality dimension that prods us as to how our story is going and a quality dimension that has something to do with our contact with our story and our awareness of it, and these quality dimensions seem to have a relationship to each other. How do we judge how our story is going? Whence the vague sense of failure or the sense of satisfaction that lies basically beneath the ups and downs or feeling that all's right with our world? Story seems to go before everything. It seems to stand as a criterion from the beginning. Long before we learn to analyze, all our choices to act or not to act tell a story. That story seems to break itself up into many streams and subplots, but as they move by various serpentine routes and rhythms, they seem to be tending, sometimes straining against, our self-created obstacles to integration and resolution in the main plot, which has its own teleology. How well this movement is progressing seems to be information that's always available to us, even though we realize that we do not know what life will bring us next!

There is a great mystery involved in the comfort or discomfort each of us feels with his or her story. For a time one may try to live a story that doesn't quite fit. One may play at being a clown, or a wife, or a workaholic, or a bricklayer, or a drifter, or a bartender, or a cleric, or a hedonist, or a doormat. One may move in and out of ill-fitting stories, but all the while, there is a quality dimension that must be repressed if one is to stay put and stem a vague or strong sense of uneasiness with oneself. There is a risk, when one is on this razor's edge of losing oneself, as Jung found in the derangements that come when one loses touch with one's own story.

There is something, it seems, to which one must be true. "To thine own self be true," Shakespeare said. Thomas Aquinas, following Aristotle, said "Action follows being." That there are stories written into us is an ancient insight. That there is a unique story written into each of us that must be played out if we are to live fully and wholly is an insight that needs special attention in today's widespread alienation. "Our sense of meaning resides within us; it does not inhere in any extension of us that can be amputated by the wheel of fortune."[3] The Self forms a core of mysterious potential as a unique image of God. The Self defines what each of us is and pro-

vides the Who, the Why, the Whence, and the Whither of our existence.

> The meaning of life is indeed objective when it is reached, but the
> way to it is by a path of subjectivities. It requires a series of pro-
> found experiences within the privacy of the personality. The
> meaning of life cannot be told; it has to happen to a person.[4]

We both invent and discover our own stories. There is a drive to
be true to our own story and not someone else's possibilities. From
conception and birth, there exists not only a genetic code that will
actualize itself, but also a potential story to be created and discovered. God is utterly involved in each of our stories because God is
the great story and each of us is a story of God. Each of us tells the
story of God in a unique way. If I try to live some other story, no
matter how heroic, I am not being true to my personal mission to
reflect an image of God in that unique way.

> The metaphor that is most appropriate here is that of the seed. In
> the seed there is the latent potentiality of development that carries
> all the possibilities of what the full-grown species can become.
> Following this metaphor, the fullness of the oak tree is latent in
> the acorn. It is implicit there, and correspondently, the depths of
> man, his unconscious, is the carrier of human potentialities. It
> contains the possibilities of human development that are present
> in the individual but are not visible because they have not yet be-
> come manifest in life. We cannot see them until they begin to un-
> fold and fulfill themselves in the world. For this it is necessary that
> the individual develop the capacity of perceiving the inward
> process of his growth while it is in motion and before it is fulfilled.
> As he becomes sensitive to it and attunes himself to the process of
> his growth inwardly, he is able to draw his potentialities forward.[5]

Our story moves forward as we strive to be true to our own potential. At the same time, the Self is *of* and *for* all other selves and the
whole universe. The universe and the earth, too, seem to have a
story they are telling, a potential they are unfolding. We sense in
our own inner meaning that everything in the universe has its alpha
and omega. We live our story within that larger story. To live in
faith, hope, and love is to lie in this kind of connectedness with each
aspect of our own story and the story of the earth and its context. It
is to be in the process of the earth and its population, the universe

and its becoming. It is to believe in their meaningfulness, to dream dreams for them, and to add to them the care and light of our own becoming and process. In turn, the earth and its people give their meaning to our own life. As we learn more and more about roots and the story of this earth and universe, we push our own story back as far as it can go and learn more about ourselves.

### Knowing One's Story

Each of us tells a story, even if it is an unexamined life, a drifting life, a story of storylessness. This brings us to another aspect of quality. That is the quality of the relationship of awareness one has to one's story. While no one escapes telling a story merely by making choices and living life, many escape any depth of awareness of the story that their own life is telling. Life becomes for them "one damn thing after another," held together by an uncomfortable feeling of helplessness in the face of onrushing events. Modern life, with its incredibly multiple possibilities for mobility and interaction, can "fast-forward" reality, blurring contact with reality and contact with one's memories, hopes, and dreams by the sheer force of the multiplicity of experience and the erosion of Sabbaths for storytelling. We need to stop and listen for a few minutes to the voices that run through our minds, and then tell the stories we hear.

Stories are told in beginnings, middles, and ends. "We learn to see and feel profoundly when we integrate all that we have been and hope to be into the present moment without severing either memories of the past or visions of the future."[6] Each moment holds within itself all we have seen and have experienced and what we are yet to become and experience and it yields this in the process of storytelling. Psychiatry and psychology have made us aware of what we have always known, that each person needs to tell his or her story. Each of us needs to hear spoken aloud the scenarios we have created; each of us needs to affirm his or her being and the acts that have proceeded from that being. Each of us needs listeners.

Friendship has been the ancient ear for such disclosures, the place where all the events of a life can be relived, remembered, and reevaluated. We need to tell our stories to those who can hear any part of them and who will still accept all we are. But we even need to tell our plots and sub-plots to those who will listen in a less understanding way. We need to hear our story told differently to less friendly ears so that we can see our story from different angles. We need many perspectives on our story.

Writing one's story has always been another option. Diaries and journals have a long and respected history. Autobiographies are fascinating to an audience and one never gets bored writing or reading one's own autobiography.

There is always a need for being deeply aware of and in touch with one's ongoing story and such verbalization can lead to deeper awareness of the story and draw its potentialities forward. However, it is never more important to be in touch with one's story than in the midst of the mid-life crisis or during the period of the mid-life transition. At this moment, when the peril of foreclosure or regression is so real, and when a crisis of present feelings can cause emotional shipwreck, a person desperately needs to get in contact and reconnect with the widest possible life context. One needs to draw on all the strengths of the past and the potential of the future and focus them on the bumpy present, so that the reality of one's present story can sustain one through the hiatus between the first and second halves of life and direct one through an authentic transition.

Like a high jumper, it is necessary to move back first before taking the leap into the second half of life. Faith demands that we embrace our human history, not sidestep, ignore, or nostalgically long over it. At this time it is important to see the past in order to own it. In recording this personal history in journals and dialogues, a person can awaken within the Self all the riches that the past has incorporated, all the unsung blessings, all the evils and misfortunes that have been lived through and overcome.

> The initial focus in the mid-life transition is on the past. The major task is to reappraise the life structure or the Settling Down period, within the broader perspective of early adulthood as a whole and even of pre-adulthood. A man's review of the past goes on in the shadow of the future. His need to reconsider the past arises in part from a heightened awareness of his mortality and a desire to use the remaining time more wisely. Past and future coexist in the present but he suffers from a corrosive doubt that they can be joined.[7]

One needs to see how one's story breaks itself up. What are the chapters of one's life? Keeping a journal is an excellent way to do the ground work on this. Ira Progoff has created a dynamic journaling process that mirrors the life processes and is a road map through the inner world of story.[8] In his method, the periods or chapters are the stepping stones of one's life. Each time a period is evoked, it presents itself colored by the accent of the present. At mid-life, when mortality is pressing heavily and half of life has passed, the chapters are bound to present themselves in particularly significant ways.

One must look closely at each chapter. In each one what were the settings, the people, the visions, the hurts, the joys, the guilts, the quests for meaning, the image of God? One must take a long time with this story and come at it from as many different perspectives as possible. Following Progoff's method, one could write a dialogue with others, and in a relaxed state of consciousness allow the person one is writing to answer on paper. Such a dialogue from one's inner Self reveals more than one thinks one knows. Since every part of our lives is personalized by our personal connection with it, every event, task, community, place, and dream can be personified and can speak to us as our pen records such dialogues. One can return to the chapters in other ways as well. The people from the past who are still living and who can shed light on vague memories may profitably be consulted. Places may be visited. Imagination and memory can bring us through past days and rooms and faces, and feelings long forgotten can be relived.

Work may need to be done to deal with unresolved grief. Professional help may be needed to work through repressed anger and latent sorrows. But one can ordinarily face the past with all its problems aware that whatever it held, one has reached this place, and the strength one now possesses has been acquired in the process of dealing with that past.

One needs to get in touch once again with one's past enthusiasms and the images of oneself that once drew all of life's energy toward them and set one on a new road in life. The image of oneself as an artist or a prophet or a homemaker or a businessman once came as an interior experience and was the basis for a new unit of life experience.

> In this unit the image that carried the original visionary feeling of possibility increasingly becomes dominant as it sets the direction

for the events that take place within that unit and spreads a sense
of purpose through all its parts. Thus, the dominant image serves
an integrative role in the unit of experience.[9]

Continuity is part of the nature of the process of human life, and
what once was so important may still offer a key to one's story, one's
Self, even if at the time of mid-life crisis one sees the earlier image
as a present curse that has brought one now to rage and regret. A
possible way to become unstuck is to reawaken that part of the
story, that image, with the joys, excitement, and energies of the
past.

In rummaging through one's past story one may come across a
neglected "pearl of great price." There were choices made in
preference to other options one once had, which may now be open
possibilities for the future. One needs to return to these forks in the
road.

> Those untaken roads contain the experiences of our life that have
> remained unlived. . . . These unlived possibilities of life have
> never been given their chance; yet many of them have been car-
> ried silently in the depth of us year after year waiting for a new op-
> portunity. They are capacities of life that were by passed because
> of the pressures of our existence, but many of them retain the
> strength of life and await the appropriate moment for being given
> form and expression.[10]

As the closets of the past open to reveal the ugliness and sin others
have inflicted or the crimes of one's own past, a great work of reconciliation is necessary so that one can move forward unencumbered
by a suppressed and repressed guilt and bitterness. It is important
to see that forgiving others or oneself is not a matter of "sweeping
the dirt back under the rug" with a benign word. One needs to look
at and face destructiveness in the larger context of one's whole life.
What good has come out of this evil? One may ask that kind of
question only after allowing oneself to feel anger, hurt, and out-
rage, or guilt, shame and deep sorrow at the evil. One can accept or
give forgiveness only after one has really confronted and wrestled
with it in all its baseness. In the external, physical world, those evils
will never be undone. They have made their sick contribution to the
history of the world's evil. Yet in the inner world of spirit, evil can
be transformed into strength, compassion, reparation, wisdom,

new life, and direction. These undoubtedly have a contribution to make to the history of the world as well.

These parts of one's story need verbalization, symbolization, and ritual so that the new spirit can be given body. Alcoholics Anonymous uses storytelling and its sponsor system and self-sacrificing communal support in this way. The Jewish rituals of Yom Kippur and the Christian sacrament of reconciliation are in a long line of the human need to externalize conversion.

No one reaches the age of forty without experiencing human destructiveness. Discussing the individual's need to integrate the creativity — destructiveness polarity at mid-life, Levinson writes:

> His developmental task is to understand the place of destructiveness in his own life and in human affairs generally. Much of the work of this task is unconscious. What is involved above all is the reworking of painful feelings and experiences. Some men articulate their new awareness in words, others in the esthetic terms of music, painting or poetry. Most men simply live it out in their daily lives. In any case, a man must come to terms with his grievances and guilts, his view of himself as victim and villain in the continuing tale of man's inhumanity to man.[11]

Owning our own history is crucial to evoking hope in mid-life. Unless we can discover the good in our past despite whatever tragic events affected our lives, there is little chance of evoking expectations for the future. We need to treat ourselves as Jesus treated the people he met. With him there were no outcasts. The Samaritan Woman[12] with her rather questionable life-style was first accepted and then gently, step-by-step, led to own her history, "the five men," and her deepest questions and longings for the Messiah, the Savior. In her excitement at her discovery of the Savior, she was saved. She left her former self-image at the well with her bucket and ran to the townspeople (who well knew her story) as a prophet and herald of the total acceptance of Jesus. With Zacchaeus the thief, Jesus follows the same pattern. First there is acceptance: "Come down, tonight I will stay with you."[13] Then Zacchaeus becomes able to see himself as a philanthropist who will give half of his property to the poor and, in addition, make fourfold restitution to his victims. It is Jesus this time who says it: "Today salvation has come to this house."[14] Jesus shows us a God who loves us not after we are all "cleaned up" but a God who loves and accepts us first. As we look into the early parts of our past, we must sit beside the woman from Samaria, Zacchaeus, and all those others in the great Christian myths of forgiveness. Like them, we must examine our past under the assuring gaze of Jesus and the God he revealed.

Personal journals and sharing our stories with others allow us to make the journey into the past and discover the myths that have formed us and the myths we have been living. This process will lead us to discover God's action in our ongoing creation and the activation of our power to be co-creators in the ongoing creation of the Self. Just as no one reaches the age of forty without the experiences of human destructiveness, no one reaches the age of forty without having experienced the intrusion of Mystery in one's life. Some name the Mystery "God." The motto that Jung had engraved over the door of his home could head each person's story. "Called or not called, God shall be there."[15] Jung's reflection that his work led him to find the pattern of God in every person's life[16] could be a directive to the person trapped in the heart of mid-life crisis. Look for the traces of God in one's story. Whatever name one gives such experiences, everyone seems to be able to recall moments that are memorable, the source of many decisions and the source of new integration. The struggles of life are punctuated with these free gifts, these graced moments when the pattern of new creation, the pattern of God, surfaced. Abraham Maslow calls them peak experiences.[17] Gregory Baum calls them depth or religious experiences.[18] Baum points out that in this age what has classically been described as the religious experiences of the holy seems to be rare[19] while experiences he designates as secular religious or depth experiences are more universal. Research from Andrew Greely and William McCready indicates that the experience of ecstasy or what could be called the holy is not so rare at all.

> In the research that McCready and I are doing . . . there is evidence that one-half of the American population would report having experiences or union with "a powerful spiritual force that draws me out of myself." About one-fifth would report frequent such experiences. We may conclude, tentatively at least, that the capacity for transient episodes of ecstasy is widespread in the population.[20]

As one tells one's story, one may recall the power of an experience of the holy or discover for the first time that one has had such experiences without naming them. William James describes such experiences with four characteristics:

Ineffability: Such an experience defies expression, conceptualization and verbalization.

Noetic Quality: A knowing, a way of understanding and seeing with fantastic clarity.

Transiency: Quickly passing.

Passivity: Another power seems to grasp one.[21]

People use the words awe, wonder, humility, peace, or wisdom to describe their subjective reactions in the midst of and in the wake of ecstasy.

There are other religious or depth experiences which Baum calls secular that can be found in one's past. Those are the experiences that stand out above time and space, above the dull, grey-tinged hours of one's story. They are experiences of *encounter* when another person touched our lives and made us grow. It could have been an author or a lecturer, or someone we met only briefly, who said a word that was made flesh in us, a person who saw a gift in us and gave it wings, a person who saw and healed a flaw in us. Perhaps it was a person like Nathan in the Hebrew Scriptures who pierced David to his guilty heart when he said: "That man is you."[22]

There were religious experiences of *communion, friendship, love* when we may have recognized our own lovableness in the eyes of another. There were experiences of *protest* when we were moved to righteous indignation and action at the injustice done to an individual or a people. There were experiences of *solidarity* with other human beings and with the universe. There were experiences of *beauty* when the evil and ugliness of the world were swallowed in a gasp at a sunset or a symphony. There were religious experiences out of the questions we asked on the collapse of our dreams, or idols, or morals, or on the betrayal of a friend, or the shock of our own power to betray.

If we go to our story with the intention of finding where God has been overtly active in our lives, we may come to a new experience of awe and wonder. We will certainly begin to be in touch with the dynamism that is in the depths of our life, the story of God that is being told. We may even touch the ultimate perception that we have been and are infinitely loved and led.

As we write or tell these stories of our religious experiences of God's action in our lives, we will be doing what the Scriptures attempt to do. They try to put into words God's action in people's lives. In the Scriptures, as often as in our own lives, encounters with God take place in most unlikely situations. Moses first met God and discovered his own mission to reflect the image of God by freeing his people not in the burning bush experience but in his religious experience of *protest*. Moses met the liberator God when in a rage he killed the overseer who was torturing a Hebrew slave.

The magnificent attempts to express these ineffable encounters with God that happened to Miriam, Joseph, Samuel, Isaiah, Jesus shed light on our lives as we read them.

### Myth and Story

The Hebrew and Christian Scriptures constitute one of the most powerful mythic systems in history. We must, however, understand the word myth in the right way. Myths are great poems. They are doorways to wonder, to the experience of the holy. Myths do not speak primarily of historic events that have occurred, but of themes of the inner world of imagination. They arise out of permanent and universal elements of our human spirits. They are misread when they are seen as "mere untruths" or as primitive historical tales. Myths, when they are alive and continue to make contact with the inner Self from which they originally spring, have great power to vivify a person. This is because they exhibit universal features, matters fundamental to ourselves, and messages to the conscious mind from the collective unconscious.

> Like the nest of a bird, a mythology is fashioned of materials drawn from the local environment, apparently altogether unconsciously but according to an architecture unconsciously dictated from within.[23]

Myths lead one to believe in the *possibility* of a solution, which is even more important to living life than actually *finding* a solution. When in mid-life one reaches the end of naivete, one can swing to the other side and become confirmed in cynicism. Such hopelessness can be paralyzing. One desperately needs the motivation to imagine solutions. Einstein imagined. Translated into the language of the Christian mythological system, belief in the possibility of solution would be at the core of the Gospel: the coming of the Kingdom. Translated into the language of personal and spiritual growth at mid-life, this would be belief in and hope for the coming of the Kingdom in one's own life.

At the center of our lives there must be an ongoing, creative tension between our personal stories and the mytholical stories of our race, between our personally and culturally shared myths. The great myths provide the common images embodied in the unique story of every person. "A myth is a large controlling image that gives philosophical meaning to the facts of ordinary life."[24]

When the Hebrew-Christian myths are read mystically and not literally, they are worthy of the best of humanity, eminently large images. People may intensify faith, hope, and love in their own stories when Christian myths can contact and illumine those stories. The grand themes of their mythology are transpersonal and transcultural. They speak directly to the perennial mysteries of life: birth, fear, hope, death, human love, and human suffering. Myth gives new depth and meaning to life.

> The ultimate home of myths is the primordial situation of human existence . . . the ambition of myth is to become the structure of consciousness through which the human situation will be appropriated.[25]

If the cultural aspects of the Testaments are now seen critically, not literally, then the heart of these Judeo-Christian myths, which so perfectly present an image of the archetypes of humanity, will shine through. When biblical scholarship is taken into account, the human situations, the human problems behind the original text, will come to the fore. It will be unfailingly primordial human situations that ground each story.

In the mid-life transition, as one makes peace with one's past situations and problems, as one embraces one's story in the light of Christian mythology, a transcendent dimension interjects itself in the story. Something bigger than the facts of the past light them from within. It is my story in the context of an infinite story; deaths become swallowed up in resurrection, regrets and boredom in a love stronger than death. Good can be perceived in a realization of a humanity that struggles and copes and goes on. Welcome, then, is the second half of such a life, and welcome eternity.

## Notes

1. Michael Novak, *Ascent of the Mountain, Flight of the Dove* (New York: Harper and Row, 1971), p. 52.

2. Jonathan Stedall, producer, "The Story of Carl Gustav Jung," B.B.C. television documentary, filmed in 1971.

3. Roger L. Gould, *Transformations, Growth and Change in Adult Life* (New York: Simon and Schuster, 1973), p. 318.

4. Ira Progoff, *The Symbolic and the Real* (New York: McGraw-Hill, 1963), p. 14.

5. *Ibid.*, pp. 21-22.

6. Sam Keen and Anne Valley Fox, *Telling Your Story* (New York: Signet Books, 1973), p. 14.

7. Daniel J. Levinson, *The Seasons of a Man's Life* (New York: Ballantine Books, 1978), p. 192.

8. Ira Progoff, *At a Journal Workshop* (New York: Dialogue House Library, 1975), p. 9.

9. Ira Progoff, *The Practice of Process Meditation* (New York: Dialogue House, 1980), p. 56.

10. Progoff, *At a Journal Workshop*, p. 135.

11. Levinson, *The Seasons of a Man's Life*, pp. 223-24.

12. John 4:1-42.

13. Luke 19:5.

14. Luke 19:9.

15. Jonathan Stedall, B.B.C. Documentary.

16. *Ibid.*

17. Abraham Maslow, *Religions, Values and Peak Experiences* (New York: Viking Press, 1964), p. 19, note.

18. Gregory Baum, *Faith and Doctrine* (New Jersey: Paulist Press, 1969), p. 59.

19. *Ibid.*, p. 67.

20. Andrew M. Greeley, *Ecstasy: A Way of Knowing* (New York: Englewood Cliffs, N.J.: Prentice-Hall, 1979), p. 11.

21. William James, *The Varieties of Religious Experience* (New York: The New American Library, 1958), pp. 292-93.

22. 2 Sam. 12:7.

23. Joseph Campbell, *Myths to Live By* (New York: Bantam Books, 1973), p. 223.

24. Mark Schorer, "The Necessity of Myth," *Myth and Mythmaking*, ed. Henry A. Murray (New York: George Braziller, 1960), p. 355.

25. Shea, *Stories of God*, pp. 52-53.

# 7

## Prayer:
## A Way of Dealing
## with Mid-life Crisis
## and Transition

### Faith and Prayer

The crisis of mid-life is a faith crisis. The transition is to rebirth. To move on, one has to believe. If one is to be reborn to living in a new way, one has to believe that one is, and is worth being. One has to believe in living. Before the yawning graves of those who forty years ago were the giants who peopled one's world, before the death of one's youthful body and dreams, one has to believe that one still exists and that it is worth returning from these cemeteries of such obvious concrete futility. Before one can be reborn to new life with new-found meanings, values, goals, before one can even begin to repattern a life that flows more truly from the true inner self, one has to find faith; one has to get in touch with the less obvious structures of belief within, with the symbols that will channel energy toward birthing and continue to channel energy toward rebuilding.

The language of aspiration and transcendence has always been prayer. The attitude for this impregnation and pregnancy has always been retreat. The language and the attitude both effect and express faith and rebirth. Prayer is a human thing to do. People have, it seems, always prayed. They have always retreated. Sleep itself seems to be a simple, instinctual form of prayer. It is a retreat from the external world to an inner self, which opens beyond time and space and reveals itself in symbols. The prayer of primitive people seemed to incorporate and externalize these elements and add an awareness of relationship. Judeo-Christian prayer incor-

114

porates all these, and adds the awareness of the Other as infinitely more than space, eternally more than time, and utterly benevolent. Specifically, Christian prayer is an Incarnational perception of all of this. God with one is an enfleshment, a daily and continous event, adverted to or not. Consciously present or unconsciously present — always passionately loving and longing for love, Christian prayer is adverting to and being present to God. It is opening oneself to that increasing presence and love. Augustine wrote, "You have made us for yourself, O God, and our hearts are restless until we rest in you." This image is filled with magnetic power. It draws pure faith to itself. Once identified with it, it draws faith in the Self and in living to itself. The advice of the religions to one who has never been able to believe in such a God has always been to pray to that God, to act as if one did believe, to act out in love and cry out in prayer as if there were such a God. For those who have believed, but whose faith-life has been expressed only implicitly, mid-life transition becomes a moment of call to conversion and prayer, because prayer can be a way through the storm and an essential element in a dynamic mid-life period.

Prayer is a means of transcendence. It is a way out. The whole human organism cries out for meaning. Meaning is always beyond and more than the microcosm of the individual. Only when the individual dies to itself does it become more. Death to oneself is death to one's ego, which is the center of the universe. At mid-life, that ego is in death throes, needing desperately to be reborn in a union with the true Self. The true Self finds its origin in being an image of the Creator. Such a myth about the Self gives it transcendent meaning. Prayer is the way to let that meaning soak into the whole personality. Through prayer one comes to the self by recognizing its existence in something far greater. One is with that possibility and it becomes the only reality.

When, one day in mid-life, one comes to doubt oneself and all one's relationships and commitments, and when the pain and anxiety of this dragging away of psychic energy from all that formerly was so life-giving begins to overwhelm, there surfaces the depth question: Why bother? Lucky the one who lets that question stand; the one who has let all the pain and all the doubt surface; the one who has not drowned the doubt in alcohol or smothered it in drugs or hyperactivity. That question is a prayer. It asks for meaning from beyond. It looks for an answer. It is the underside of faith and rebirth.

Agony at mid-life before the now more clearly seen rottenness in oneself, in the others who people one's world, at the crushing ugliness of the social fabric that rises from the streets, or from the airwaves in the car, or from the violent world of T.V. in the living room, is the underside of faith. This agony is an awareness of what should be, what might be. This agony is a depth questioning. It, too, is prayer. It can be the way through to mature aspiration and transcendence. Aspiration is both a human and a godly thing. At twenty, aspiration has a world to conquer. At forty, aspiration has been somewhat beaten back by the world, with all its death and evil. At forty, aspiration has to look through beyond that world and the conquering self who is in so much pain. It looks for ultimates.

The language of suffering and of aspiration has always been prayer. To pray is to say "yes" to God, but it is also an impassioned questioning of life, of death, of evil, and of God, which affirms the contradiction we experience in how we know it "ought" to be and how it actually is (or seems ? to be).

> I am overcome by my trouble. I am distraught by the noise of the evening because of the oppression of the wicked . . . my heart is in anguish within me. The terrors of death have fallen upon me and horror overwhelms me. And I say, "O, that I had wings like a dove!" But I call upon God. And the Lord will save me.[1]

This prayer of the psalmist might well be the cry of one in mid-life crisis. The regret, the anger, the doubt, the negative feelings of the crisis, the desire to run away from one's life, self, and relationships are all there. Verbalizing the pain in the presence of the God of the Kingdom, the God of how things "ought" to be, turning to the One who offers rest, the One toward whom one's restless heart aspires, anticipates and can effect faith in oneself and one's life again. In calling and looking outward toward the Other, one ceases to be locked up in oneself and in the relationships that are often a painful source of suffering or indifference at this time. In looking into the mirror of the Infinite Being—truth, love, goodness, beauty—one sees one's reflection; one gets a glimpse of the true Self; a hint, a rumor that there is such a true Self and that it is ultimately good. In that is a glimmer of new faith and provides direction to the search for the true Self in the journey-aspiration of the second half of life.

In such prayer, it is also implied that one cannot come to a realization of the true Self by one's own efforts. Transpersonal psychologists tell us we must always remain open to the energies of the universe. In Judeo-Christian terms, one needs to constantly open one's self to the gift of self-realization and self-transcendence, which is graciously and gratuitously offered to the human race by its Author, who first loves each of its members. Prayer is a gift because it is inborn.

### The Way to Prayer

For the believer, especially at mid-life, there is no opposition between opening oneself to the energies of the universe and opening oneself to the grace of the God of all.

> It is the human experience which is the starting point of prayer: a process of growing awareness of why people love us and forgive us, and of openness to the wonder and glory of creation, of nature and of the elements. Frequently, in that endless search for peace and stillness, we look toward big old established parts of creation—the sea, the mountains, the countryside. Here we discover great beauty, natural stillness and the constant reassuring motion of a life-giving force behind things.[2]

At mid-life, each person needs to find what it is that brings him or her into the attitude of retreat and the expression and the language of prayer. Such retreats into prayer can last an instant, or an hour, or a month, or longer. To pray, one does not need God language or words at all. The mid-life person has had enough life experience to know this. In mid-life one can be well beyond externalism. At this mid-life stage, people can look back and recognize true moments of prayer, whether they happened inside or outside the auspices of a particular religion or religious language. Sometimes one sees clearly that some of one's past "prayer" was, in fact, something else, while other experiences were one's best prayer. In examining one's story, one may get a glimpse of what, indeed, draws one naturally into prayer. Each personality type has its own different way.

Before looking at some possible ways into prayer, one needs to look at what constitutes praying. Prayer is affirming God and oneself. Prayer is whole-person being attentive to God, longing for God, opening to God, reaching out to God, surrendering to God, needing God, centering oneself in God, communication with God, offering oneself to God, resting in God. Prayer is an I-Thou encounter with God. Prayer is hunger for God. Prayer is active and passive; words and silence; action and stillness. As a divine human encounter, "prayer is the interiorizing of the Incarnation."[3] Prayer is solitary and communal, personal and political. Prayer is profoundly immanent and profoundly transcendent; profoundly simple and profoundly mysterious. It is a knowing of God and a "not knowing." Prayer is a retreat with God in one's conscious ego; a regression with God into the unconscious depths of the self. There is no place where prayer is impossible. There is no time when prayer is impossible. There is no way in which every person must pray.

There are ways into prayer. There are contents and agendas for prayer. It is important at mid-life to find one's own best way into prayer, a way that is compatible with one's own inner self and that focuses that self in God as it begins its important work of greater individuation and integration.

At mid-life, when the way of activity, even the active ways of praying, comes up against the wall of doubt and lethargy, rushing around and doing become impossible. Attention to the projects that filled one's life and gave one meaning flags. Still, in our western culture where extroversion, activity, the work ethic, and producing are supreme, it takes no little effort to bring oneself into contemplative prayer. Prayer is a whole-person activity; the body will be involved in this whole-person attentiveness to God. Thus, the body can help move the self into retreat and contemplation. One can, with the help of the body, create a center of peace within which the whole personality retires in God.

The mouth has always been a part of the body that initiates a prayerful state. One can voice the words of the psalmist or the written prayers of others, including all the scriptural prayers, to bring one's heart and mind to attend. Singing and chanting are ways to focus the self. Repetition of a mantra creates an atmosphere, reduces sense and emotional bombardments, and leads to repose. The mantra can be any simple phrase repeated rhythmically in harmony with one's breathing. Seven syllables are a help but not a necessity. The mantra can be personally composed (though preferably not an emotionally charged word or phrase), or a meaningful scriptural word or phrase. The rosary and litanies are time-honored Christian mantras. The mantra can gently push images out of mind or create the space for the mind to imagine scenes that involve all the faculties and arouse affectivity. From the mouth can come sighs or groans or the babbling, meaningless praise of what is called the "gift of tongues."

The ears and the activity of hearing can bring one to the whole-person attentiveness of deep prayer. Listening to music, with or without words, whether it be designated as sacred or not, can be a vehicle for centering. Listening to falling rain, or to birds singing, or to children at play, or to the enthusiasm of young people, or to the sound of waves, a waterfall, or a brook, or to the spoken words of Scripture can lead one to prayer, and can be a form of deep prayer. Listening to the sounds in the silence can build a cathedral around a person in a dingy room.

Seeing as well as hearing can be a way into prayer, which becomes prayer itself. Focusing on the light of a candle, or a meadow, or an ocean, or mountain, or a beautifully shaped object, is looking with eyes that see. Watching a spider spinning a web or ants building an anthill, or people in an airport can be praying. Going out to look at what tiny or great wonders are in one's own backyard, looking around at the colors and shapes and textures indoors or outdoors can engage the body, mind, and spirit in deep contemplation in the presence of the Lord of all. Gazing at a painting or a mandala or a yantra like a cross or a circle are ancient ways of presence. The word "meditation" can describe any of these activities, as well as a more cognitive activity. Meditation and the prayer that is its fruit are ways of presence. "Meditation is concerned with the development of 'presence,' a modality of being which may be expressed or developed in whatever situation the individual may be involved."[4] Prayer situates that presence in the Presence. One can steal into this Presence by dwelling on a tiny leaf or on the vast horizon or the infinity of space.

The whole body, in deliberate stillness or different motions, can lead one into prayer. Gestures, yoga postures, jogging, dancing, walking, sculpting are some possibilities. The great rituals and gestures of Christianity bring the whole body into an activity that is a retreat from "everydayness," and into a possibility filled with

Presence. The eucharistic liturgy, a feast for the eyes and ears and a feast of eating and drinking, is also a feast of movement from presence to Presence. It creates a deep communal atmosphere by drawing each participant into its own rhythm and movement and uniting them in a swell of prayer. As they sit, stand, kneel, offer, sign peace, process to the table, they are united as the Body of Christ to make the Body of Christ, to be the Body of Christ, to go forth as the Body of Christ. They eat and drink the Body of Christ not only from the altar; they also assimilate its reality from the community, the members in the pews, in their whole-person gestures of coming together and going forth as a community.

There is whole-person involvement in the activity of writing a journal. One can create a dialogue on paper with the Lord or with someone out of the pages of scripture or the lives of the saints that comes from the deepest center of one's self. One's prayer is written as one speaks to the other and writes the responses of the other. Writing about other aspects of one's inner life can likewise lead one to prayer. A spiritual journal is an ancient tradition. It is a memorial of inner dialogues and a way of capturing the Spirit.

Prayerful reading of scripture involves the whole person, imagining oneself in a scriptural event and reflecting on all of the persons and their reactions. Being there in one's imagination can be a profound experience. People through the centuries have cried and been filled with deep joy in this kind of mediation. The mysteries of the rosary and the stations of the cross were ways of "reading scripture" when people did not read the printed word. A few lines may be enough to lead into deep prayer. Everyone has favorite passages that write themselves upon the heart. These nourish one again and again throughout life. It is also important, however, to allow oneself to be challenged by scripture one would not oridinarily choose to read. It is to this end that many Christian churches have adopted a three-year cycle of readings. It is an amazing thing to think that people all over the world are hearing the same readings on a given Sunday. The Scriptures are the verbalization of the religious experiences of thousands of people and paint a consistent portrait of their experiences of God. By reading scripture, one can learn to recognize the God experiences of one's own life.

Focusing on one's breathing is an ancient and widespread way to prayer. The Hebrews saw breath as the breath of God. It is always a way of getting in touch with rhythm that produces profound effects. "When we harmonize our actions and our breath, breathing becomes a central regulating rhythm which gives many people a feeling of centeredness and calm."[5] Focusing on the inner movements in one's body—the inner sensations and the outer sensations of touch—can make one present to oneself in a new way. Progressive relaxation of each part of the body has the same effect. Both can become in faith a kind of prayer to the God who incarnates in each person as image of God.

All these ways through the body, whether they are through a deeper sensory awareness or sensory deprivation, shift one's cognition mode: "During meditation, the verbal logical 'self' that reasons in orderly sequence and is highly aware of time, seems to dim out. . . our 'interior speech,' that ever-present running stream of words that occupies our thinking during regular activity, is either stilled or relegated to a background role."[6] Another way of looking at the shift is one's thinking that occurs during meditation is to see it as a suspension of conscious ego control.

## The Self in Prayer

All of these means are ways of meditation or centering and can be one aspect of contemplative praying. All this is a way of describing the "I" in the I/Thou encounter. What of the "Thou"? The only way of speaking about the Thou is in symbols. The word "God" and all of our affirmations about God are symbols. God is unfathomable, unable to be reduced to a name or a notion. Because God is Other, our experience of God is always meditated, if only through the self that experiences God. Experiencing oneself as the image of God can be an awesome thing. This was the personal prayer of Jesus in a unique way, but it can be ours analogously. Yet, when the ego is very much in control, as it is in the first half of life, the Self can be opaque indeed. It is possible to experience life and not know life. It is possible to experience emotion and not know one is sad or angry or anxious. It is possible to understand many things without knowing what it is to understand, to have peak experiences without recognizing or naming them. It is possible to live life in this ensouled body and never know the transparency of the Self. It is possible to experience one's body and the world through one's own spirit and never attend to spirit. One can swim in a sea of spirit and miss it because it is too close. Like the blood in one's veins, one has no awareness of it until a gash spills it out to view. Prayer is like that gash, if it is true prayer. At mid-life, the self is very vulnerable to such a gash, and as the outer structure crumbles, as one's former meaning, values, and goals give way, the self within draws one to inwardness. The way *in* is through meditation; the way of realization of the true Self starts with prayer.

What are the agendas, the contents of such prayer? They will be awe and adoration, affirmation and gratitude, reconciliation and conversion, yearning and asking. All of these, however, in the paralysis of crisis, may take the form of wordless, dry waiting, or simple prayer of the heart.

In the sixteenth century, John of the Cross and Teresa of Avila attempted to deliniate stages of prayer, or mysticism. Teresa's description of these successive stages is recorded in her *Interior Castle*. The mansions of the Castle are stages of growth of self in God. Comparing Teresa's third mansion with Jung's description of the adult personality at the threshold of the mid-life transition yields amazing similarities:

> For the personality problems that plague the maturing adult ego as it moves toward the middle-age crisis correspond almost point for point with those encountered in the third mansion: the growing alienation of the conscious ego from a larger sense of self, effective aridity, the evaporation of a noumenal sense of mystery, the growth of largely unconscious neurotic anxieties, persona possession, rationalism and the subjection of personal growth processes to the despotic control of the ego."[7]

All this breaks down in the fourth mansion: the despotism of the ego gives way to rapprochement with the true Self, a new possibility in prayer arises, and a new center of peace within the soul regains control. Teresa calls this new prayer form the "prayer of recollection."

> At a therapeutic level, the anxieties that kept the conscious ego prisoner in the third mansion begins, as Jung suggests, to be healed. But for the contemplative, this deeper healing of memories is itself a passive grace — the point of openness to God in prayer."[8]

For Teresa, John of the Cross, and the author of the fourteenth-century *Cloud of Unknowing*, this new form of prayer of the fourth stage is a knowing that is loving. For all of these, such prayer is imageless and without abstractions. Along with the sacramental approach possible in prayer, there is another tradition that would not make imageless prayer a special peak in spiritual growth. However, Gregory of Nyssa, Augustine, and Ignatius of Loyola all emphasized the use of images. This prayer form may be particularly needed today in this rationalistic age.

> Meditation through images with the resulting externalization of these images in art, writing, weaving, sculpture, dance, etc. is a form of worship and celebration without which modern persons, with all their rational sophistication, often cannot exist as integrated joyful individuals.[9]

Images or no, abstractions or no, Christian prayer praises the Abba. This familiar name for God was shocking to Jesus' contemporaries; Jesus not only used this form of address himself, but invited others to use it. When he was asked to teach his followers to pray, he taught them to say, "Our Father." Jesus not only taught them the words of what we call the Lord's Prayer, he taught them the whole agenda of this prayer as an agenda for all praying.

"Our Father who art in heaven." The Abba is not only my father, he is father of all; if parent of all, he is mother as well. He is generativity. He shares being with all. At mid-life, each one of us needs to identify with this kind of generativity. One needs to move away from the pole of competition toward a balance of collaboration. One needs to move toward becoming more one's own true Self, the Self that is the "spitting image" of the Father, so that one can share it with the others in one's world. One who always accommodates and never frees up to realize his or her own power does not have a self to contribute in relationship. The generative person is one who not only gives himself or herself but who nurtures the fullest development of the true Self in others. Abba accepts each and all of his children unconditionally. He does not ask them to become all that can be before he will love them. He loves them first, and so empowers them with the strength to become. The generative person has this kind of approach to people. He or she doesn't wait for people to prove they are worth paying attention to. He or she attends to them first. Such openness is enriching, since people tend to blossom in the presence of someone who accepts them as they are.

Heaven is a symbol of transcendence. The Abba is beyond the rainbow, deeper than one's self, more than one can expect or imagine. The Abba in heaven is very near—closer to one than oneself—for heaven is where one is with God. Heaven is a state of being whole. Heaven is already. Heaven is where the will of God is done; where all is accomplished. Heaven is a dynamism of love. Heaven is the dream deep down in the fabric of our being that makes us scream out that things are not well, not right, not finished. We both know heaven and do not know it. At mid-life, we need to retire more and more into the heaven in the midst of our being. We need to be more at home in it so that we can bring back from each retreat into heaven the wisdom and power that dwell there and enflesh it.

"Thy Kingdom come, thy will be done on earth as it is in heaven." When we bring back from prayer the contours of the Kingdom, we need to throw our gifts into working to bring that Kingdom about. The Kingdom is God's to bring, but we are involved. We are being used to lay some foundations as we receive the blueprints from God in the heaven within. We may come to see prayer being lived in our work for the Kingdom. Some of this may take the form of protest. Jesus' life was one of protest against the evil and suffering and pain around him. His miracles were a protest. He incarnated the wholeness of the Kingdom whenever he cured the physical, emotional, or spiritual ills he encountered. The prayer of the mid-life Christian needs to be lived out in the overcoming of evil. This is political prayer. Today's injustices are woven into the social fabric, and the crushing of the innocent is carried out by great governments, corporations, institutions, even churches. Generative people grow as they pour themselves out in efforts that are so much bigger than themselves. This is a form of self-transcendence and immortality that overcomes the inertia and fear of death that have invaded the mid-life person.

"Give us this day our daily bread." This is the voicing of receptivity. It is an attitude of supplication. At mid-life, one needs to acknowledge that one is somewhat helpless. The end of naivete is not easy to accept. There is a great temptation to cynicism when one who has lived through so many experiences feels the defeat and regret of the death of one's "omnipotence." Petitionary prayer is a beautiful, comforting kind of praying. Jesus constantly must have told his disciples to ask, since such phrases as "ask and you shall receive" are repeated many times in the four Gospels. The power of positive thinking is a new way of speaking about this prayer of dreaming about God, and of what one wants and needs daily for oneself and others. Such praying is self-programming to be mindful of the daily needs of others.

"Forgive us our trespasses as we forgive those who trespass against us." Here we encounter affirmation of mutuality. Again, we set ourself up to deal with others as we want God, the Abba, to deal with us. This forgiveness is crucially important if the mid-life person is to move on. The greatest blocks to progress and growth can come through the hardness and damming up that comes when a person refuses to forgive. Holding grudges or nurturing hostilities do more damage to the person who harbors that kind of bitterness than to the one toward whom the bitterness is directed. Forgiveness, however, is very difficult. One must know that one is always being loved and forgiven by the Abba in order to possess the power to forgive another. One needs to let the Father's love flow through one to the other. One needs to lift the gates that are stopping that love and allow one's own fragile love and forgiveness to flow out with that of the Father. Mid-life is a special moment to make this kind of peace with the past so that one can pick up the pieces of one's life and move into the future.

"Lead us not into temptation but deliver us from evil." This is the need of the realist at mid-life. Evil is very powerful, and within, and all around—one knows this now. One needs to keep touching base with the good within and around. One needs to keep reminding oneself that there is a force more powerful than any evil and that it is preoccupied with one's well-being. Such faith provides tremendous power to move into the future knowing that nothing can separate one from the love of the Father, and so nothing can ultimately imprison or destroy one.

If mid-life presents one with a faith crisis, praying in this manner, constantly remembering that the Kingdom, Power and Glory are within one's reach and as close as a prayer can carry one safely through the storm. When one thinks one cannot pray, when one thinks one does not believe, one is told by the Christian

Scriptures that the Spirit within cries out "Abba." Called or not, God is there, and even the wish that God be there is the prayer that will suffice.

## Notes

1. Ps. 55: 4A, 5, 17.

2. Kenneth Leach, *True Prayer* (San Francisco: Harper and Row, 1980), p. 4.

3. *Ibid.*

4. Claudio Naranjo, *The Domain of Meditation: What Is Meditation?* ed. John White (New York: Doubleday, 1974), pp. 17–18.

5. Patricia Carrington, *Freedom in Meditation* (New York: Doubleday, 1977), p. 305.

6. *Ibid.*, p. 306.

7. Donald L. Gelpi, *Experiencing God* (New York: Paulist Press, 1978), p. 334.

8. *Ibid.*, p. 336.

9. Morton Kelsey, *Transcend: A Guide to the Spiritual Quest* (New York: Crossroad, 1981), p. 156.

# 8
# A Mid-life Task:
# Projection of the Future

I once attended a symposium on hope at which James Carroll was one of the celebrated speakers. Carroll was speaking of the crisis of the Church. Many Roman Catholics had evolved into a theology of the Church that in no way was being experienced in church structures, institutions, or norms. There was (and is) an ever-widening discrepancy between theology and praxis. Speaking of this matter and the crisis it reflected, Carroll said the one hope we have of being lifted out of the stalemate and its destructiveness is the "utilization of imagination."

Imagination is one of the distinctive qualities of our humanity. Without its use we are less than human. Without its use we cannot transcend ourselves and we are left to our own devices. Without its use we cannot go beyond ourselves or experience being another. Without it we have no God to love and we cannot love our neighbor as we love ourselves. There is something deeply and genuinely religious about imagination. The crucial need of the utilization of imagination in the life of the Church was also acknowledged by Karl Rahner: "The future of the Church in Germany cannot be planned and built up merely by the application of generally recognized Christian principles; it needs the courage of an ultimately charismatically inspired, creative imagination."[1]

Fear of our imagination has been instilled in many of us since childhood, as was fear of our sexuality, our emotions, our uniqueness. I remember giving a workshop to a group. One of the goals of the workshop was to facilitate the contacting of each one's unique gifts and how each one would like to use those gifts to make a personal contribution to building up the world (the Kingdom of God) and the Church. We brainstormed on the troubles and needs of the

127

world (racism, poverty, the aged, sexism, threat of nuclear war, our prisons, etc.) and of the Church (sexism, stalemate on ecumenism, materialism, crisis of authority, clericalism, institutionalism, etc.). After the brainstorming, I requested the participants to imagine themselves responding to the needs of the world or the needs of the Church to which they felt called. I suggested that we allow the Spirit to use our imagination and to fantasize that we are wholeheartedly responding to one of these crucial needs. One person actually jumped up and called out in anger, "I do not believe in fantasy. Using your imagination is something I was taught not to do."

How true those words were. And yet the great people of history have not been afraid of their imagination. Martin Luther King said, "I have a dream." Today we see his dream slowly, painfully coming to reality. Daring to dream, to imagine another way, sows the seeds of change. Some hated him for daring to dream, others loved him for it. "Now Joseph had a dream and he repeated it to his brothers. . . And they hated him still more, on account of his dream and of what he said."[2]

Lack of imagination locks us into the present. "The creative person tends to see the limitations of the present as not final. He [or she] is concerned with alternatives. The unimaginative see the future as an extension of the present and define their future in terms of fitting into present structures."[3] Such an attitude is death to creativity and the life of the Spirit in the individual and in society.

In *Saint Joan*, George Bernard Shaw's classic play about Joan of Arc, the English interrogate Joan about her actions and the mission she proclaimed:

English: What did you mean when you said that St. Catharine and St. Margaret talked to you everyday?

Joan: They do.

English: What are they like?

Joan: I will tell you nothing about that: they have not given me leave.

English: But you actually see them; and they talk to you just as I am talking to you.

Joan: No: it is quite different. I cannot tell you: you must not talk to me about my voices.

English: How do you mean? Voices?

Joan:      I hear voices telling me what to do. They come from
           God.
English:   They come from your imagination.
Joan:      Of course. That is how the message of God comes to
           us.[4]


The Scriptures bear witness to Joan's claim: "That is how the
message of God comes to us."

Having lost contact with our personal power and faculty of
fantasy and imagination, we have lost contact with our humanity,
our birthright, and our religious tradition. Both the Hebrew Scriptures and the Christian Testament give witness to the religious
tradition of fantasy and imagination.

Listen to Isaiah as the messianic poem tells (with the use of
fantasy and imagination) what it will be like when the Messiah
comes.

> The wolf lives with the lamb,
> the panther lies down with the kid,
> calf and lion cub feed together
> with a little boy to lead them.
> The cow and the bear make friends,
> Their young lie down together.
> The lion eats straw like the ox.
> The infant plays over the cobra's hole;
> into the viper's lair
> the young child puts his hand.
> They do not hurt, no harm,
> on all my holy mountain,
> for the country is filled with the
> knowledge of Yaweh
> as the waters swell the sea.[5]

Following the rich tradition of imagery in Isaiah, the book of
Revelation pictures the completion of the messianic age.

Then I saw a new heaven and a new earth; the first heaven and
the first earth had disappeared now, and there was no longer any
sea. I saw the holy city, and the new Jerusalem, coming down
from God out of heaven, as beautiful as a bride all dressed for her

husband. Then I heard a loud voice call from the throne, "You see this city? Here God lives among men. He will make his home among them; they shall be his people, and He will be their God; His name is God-with-them. He will wipe away all tears from their eyes; there will be no more death, and no more mourning or sadness."[6]

"The word poet means 'maker,' and God, the First Poet—in his special, direct revelation, the Bible—set his stamp of approval on the imaginative mode of perceiving truth. . . ."[7] It seems that it is true to our religious tradition to perceive ourselves made in the "image and likeness" of our Creator as people rich in imagery. Imagery touches the heart of the matter, the depths of human yearning and hoping. The imagery and language that Jesus used, as depicted in the gospels of Matthew, Mark, and Luke, "indicates lines along which His imagination had grown and revealed itself.[8]

Jerusalem, Jerusalem—How often have I longed to gather your children, as a hen gathers her brood under her wings, and you refused![9]

The Kingdom of heaven may be compared to a king who gave a great feast for his son's wedding.[10]

How happy are you who are poor: yours is the kingdom of God. Happy are you who are hungry now: you shall be satisfied. Happy are you who weep now: you shall laugh.[11]

Who is my mother? Who are my brothers? And stretching out his hand towards his disciples he said, Here are my mother and my brothers. Anyone who does the will of my Father in heaven, he is my brother and sister and mother.[12]

We must revere every minute aspect of ourselves and play favorites with none. Our full humanity demands this and our call to integration and wholeness makes us reach out to every neglected part of our being. Whatever our personal and communal futures are to be, they will be the result of our creative imagination or our lack of imagination. Imagination is not only the key to the present crisis of the Church, as Carroll tells us; it is the key to the crisis of the mid-life transition of each individual and to every crisis. Harvey Cox defines fantasy (so closely allied to imagination) as "the faculty for envisioning alternative life situations."[13] This, then, is the key to the social crisis of world hunger and the personal crisis of the transition of mid-life: imagining a new way of being.

It is imagination that invited the Jewish Jesus to call God "Father, Abba," and urge us to do the same. It was imagination that urged Jesus to challenge the extroverted populace to find "the kingdom of God within you." It is imagination that liberates the mid-life person from the structures each has created that no longer give life by presenting alternatives. Sometimes imagination can help us to find the way to breathe new life into deadening structures without shattering them. It is imagination that is the key to discovering the structures that will best allow the individual to be his or her true Self, to be a sacrament or outward sign of the inner reality of the genuine Self. Harmony and unification of inner and outer personal life is the ongoing process of the second half of life. It is a slow and liberating movement toward making the inside and outside the same.

If imagination is a key to the liberation of the human person locked into images of the self that were lived out in the first half of life and the structures built around those images, then imagination is not a flight into falsehood. "Imagination reveals a new level of inner reality. It does not create these elements. Imagination is a source of knowledge, a means of cognition which can dry up if it is ignored. If one pays attention to it, however, one finds a spontaneous creative process working within."[14] In addition, fantasy is not necessarily a flight into the unreal but a turning to a truth, a discovery of a greater reality of the Self. This is the purpose of the mid-life crisis and transition. We equated the aspects of the ego lived out in the first half of life with our total Self. The crisis of feelings opens me up to the reality that there is more to me trembling to be born, to breathe freely. The Mid-life transition is the time of gestation—not nine months—but close to seven or nine years. It is a bridge into the journey of the self. It is a bridge into the coming-home period of our lives. If the transition is made, we enter into the process of becoming our own true Selves. If the transition is made, we reach the turning point. The growing alienation of Self is ended and I accept my own genuine Self and the continual process of being true to it, growing in authenticity.

Carl Rogers points out that this movement toward authenticity incorporates an attention to and acceptance of my own organism.

The adaptation to the outer world and its corresponding ego development in the first half of life demanded a repression of the climate of my own organism. In order to adapt to the culture and society we alienated our own Selves. The crisis of feelings in mid-life demands a founding of the Self, a coming home, a return to the part of God's creation that is closest to us, and toward which we are most morally responsible, the Self. We must discover what we had in infancy: a unity with out own organism, a harmony with our own universe of body, mind, and spirit. The return to unity will, however, be a return not to the primitive unity of the infant but to the differentiated unity of a mature adult. This is a unity that also unites the myriad aspects of the Self in a differentiation.

This movement toward personal authenticity and unity is a return to the wisdom of our own Selves, a confidence in our own antennae, a faith in and a reverence for our own experience. The mid-life transition terminates the estrangement from the Self. Slowly, painfully we begin to pay attention to our own bodies. Our bodies know what is best for us. Our bodies know when we are in touch with our own living spirits, the life-giving waters. We each have within us a "felt sense." We have an "inner eye" that knows the way through the maze of values, goals, and projects. We drop, release the "introjected value patterns" of the culture that we mistook as our own. In the first half of life our source of evaluation was primarily outside ourselves. We wanted to win love, acceptance, and esteem and so we alienated Self and took on the values of others. In introjecting the value judgments of the culture, we lose touch with our own organismaic valuing process, we desert the wisdom of our own organism.[15] Now we are in the movement of rediscovering our own basic wisdom by owning our personal experiences and finding the locus of all evaluating within our own Selves. It is essential, Carl Rogers points out, that we come to sense and to feel what is going on within, what we are feeling, what we are experiencing, how we are reacting.[16]

As adults moving toward maturity in the second half of life, there is a tendency toward becoming more real, being our true Selves, being self-directed, fully accepting our own inner feelings, accepting the reality of process, a sensitivity toward and an acceptance of others, a greater appreciation of deep relationships, an openness toward both inner and outer experience, and a creative acceptance of the outer world. These qualities that the maturing adult exhibits point toward universal values that are not introjected, coming from outside, but are coming from within us as we move on in this process of becoming more fully human. They are the basic human values that evolve if they are allowed to and fostered. We move away from masks, pretenses, and "oughts" to a locus deep within ourselves, the core of our own Selves, and in doing so we enter our own humanity and take a giant step forward for all humanity.

In order to use the wisdom of our organism as the infant does before he or she is socialized and alienated from Self, we must discover ways to get in touch once again with our own senses, emotions, feelings, inner wisdom — the inner child within us. Gendlin, in his book *Focusing* explains it clearly. We must learn to focus within. It is within ourselves that we rediscover our own inner wisdom in contact with all our myriad parts not alienated from them. "If we want to hear what is right and good, what to think, how to act, where to turn, we need only consult our own bodies."[17] By focusing on our inner feelings and contacting our "felt sense," an inner image is formed. Creating images is the key to the unconscious and mediates the conscious and unconscious world of ours. Focusing, paying attention to a feeling within, moves us in this act of acceptance beyond the feeling. The feeling becomes, in a sense, the doorway to a movement within the Self that continues to unmake us, to change us, to enlarge our vision of Self and to engage us in the process of continual becoming. Gendlin points out our need to ackowledge that every human person has the ability to be a form maker, to create the patterns and structures that are necessary for growing authenticity. "If we accept ourselves and each other as form makers, we will no longer need to force forms on ourselves or each other."[18]

Once you are in touch with your own true Self, you have allowed your living values to emerge from your own center, your core; you have owned the powerhouse of your own imagination — you have laid the foundation for the creative process of form making that Gendlin speaks of. Your choices and decisions will flow from Self. The transition period is over and you have gone through the threshold of the second half of life and are making choices that flow from the newly discovered Self. Bernard Lonergan calls this "moral conversion": "Moral conversion changes the criterion of one's decisions and choices from satisfaction to values."[19] From this time on, we are no longer looking for the satisfaction of the approval, love, or acceptance of those outside us; instead, we search for the embodiment of the living values within the Self. In this mid-life conversion, "scales of preference shift. Errors, rationalizations, and ideologies fall and shatter to leave one open to things as they are and to man [or woman] as he [or she] should be."[20] Carl Jung also speaks of this con-version when he tells us that "Religion is nothing—if not obedience to awareness."[21] Harvey Cox counsels us to be open to "the discoveries of psychology and from the storehouse of mystical wisdom how to hear our own pulse and breath, how to reclaim our impulses, and how to feel ourselves once more from within."[22]

As we come home to the Self, we slowly terminate the transition period with the gradual emerging of a new life structure to embody the newly discovered Self. This life structure is created by free and deliberate choices. "As a transition comes to an end, it is time to make crucial choices, to give these choices meaning and commitment, and to start building a life structure around them. The choices mark the beginning of the next period. They are, in a sense, the magic product of the transition."[23] For this journeyer, in the second half of life meaning is only present when he or she is listening to the Spirit within, the inner voice. Decisions are only satisfactory when they are made in response to the inner light and revelation that subsequently comes. Our inner values and insights will determine our choices and chart our course of action. They will demand concrete embodiment and be restless until they emerge in strategies. This is a time for tearing down and building up. It is a time for personal creativity and sharply points out that living genuinely is an art. For this artistic creativity, we must accept the process of change and discernment in all the small and big seasons of life.

> There is a season for everything,
> A time for every occupation under heaven:
> a time for giving birth,
> a time for dying;
> a time for planting,
> a time for uprooting what has been planted.
> A time for killing,

a time for healing;
a time for knocking down,
a time for building.
A time for tears,
a time for laughter;
a time for mourning,
a time for dancing.
A time for throwing stones away,
a time for gathering them up;
a time for embracing,
a time to refrain from embracing.
A time for searching,
a time for losing;
a time for keeping,
a time for throwing away.
A time for tearing,
a time for sewing;
a time for keeping silent,
a time for speaking.
A time for loving,
a time for hating;
a time for war,
a time for peace.

What gain have the workers from their toil? I have seen the business that God has given to everyone to be busy with. God has everything suitable for its time; moreover God has put a sense of past and future into our minds, yet they cannot find out what God has done from the beginning to the end.[24]

As we make our future out of our choices, as we construct our life structure out of the components of our choices, we are in the religious task of entering into our ongoing creation. "The components of the life structure are not a random set of items, like pebbles washed up at the seashore. Rather, like the threads in a tapestry, they are woven into an encompassing design. Recurring themes in various sectors help to unify the overall pattern of the tapestry. Lives differ widely in the nature and patterning of the components."[25]

We have mentioned the importance of the free use of our imagination in the task of reconstructing our lives. We have mentioned focusing as a natural way of contacting our power as form makers.

Now let us look at journal writing as a process to engage ourselves in contacting our own true longings and wishes. Just as the Scriptures are often the written expression of hoped-for longings, so too our written expressions of personal longings are scriptures of the Self. When Thomas Jefferson penned, "All men are created equal," he expressed what was consciously acceptable as well as what was unconsciously longed for but unacceptable to many. "All men " consciously meant all white males in 1776 — unconsciously, it incorporated the coming freedom of the black man and the still later liberation of women, white and black. In the next two centuries, new images of the idea that "all men are created equal" would emerge from the unconscious. We too can find in our personal journals genuine seeds for our future. Through journal writing, our own unconscious emerges. The task of journal writing can create the ferment necessary for new insight and creativity. It can break open the bindings around our heart and allow us to cry out for the structure we need to be free. Keeping a journal allows us to find the new patterns for acting out our true Selves. Journal writing, like dancing, art, surfing, or any other concentated activity, creates a ritual for freedom of expression and is self-revelatory. Like focusing, it helps us to contact our felt sense and leads us into discovering its significance.

Many people find in focusing and journal writing a method of tapping the intuitive, imaginative, and creative capacity we all have. We are each called to discover the means of tapping our full potential. We have within the key to life-giving structures and creative futures. Music, art, dance, yoga, prayer of all kinds — contemplation, centering, prayer of imagination, prayer of petition — all these can tap the inner creative resources of a person.

Turmoil is always the necessary, creative ferment that issues in a transforming, creative element in our personal lives and in the world. Following turmoil, there is a need to withdraw, to become passive and allow the conscious and unconscious forces to mingle in the art of conceiving. What is conceived? It is insight. We discover the way, the authentic expression of the Self. All creative acts follow this pattern of turmoil, withdrawal, creative insight. The mid-life transition is a creative act, the artistic expression of a human life, and incorporates the turmoil of crisis, the withdrawal of the transition period, and the birth of new insight about ourselves and the meaning of our lives. The time of withdrawal is essential. It allows for and fosters a mood of quiet, intuitive attentiveness and concentration. It is a waiting period, a time of hopeful, quiet expectation that penetrates the deeper levels of the creative imagination, giving birth to genuine insight. "The theory of the creative act takes its cue primarily from the inside-identification point of view, that is, organically from the center outward, not mechanistically from the outside looking in. There, the organism is viewed as active and self-directed, not as a reactive automaton controlled by stimuli from outside."[26]

Our periods of withdrawal can be moments, hours, days, years. Learning how to relax and to let go of busyness is an important mid-life lesson. Periods of solitude and relaxation, no matter what their duration, allow us to experience our inner Selves, and in that experience of harmony that only the Self can produce, the storehouse of inner creativity is released. The Self is the archetype of wholeness. Through it we contact the power to transcend what appears to be barriers to our integration and through it we open up new vineyards for ourselves. We create the images of the future in solitude. "Your own imagery can give excellent guidance in making the choices which are best for you."[27] Solitude provides the climate for wrestling with authentic choices, for coming to terms with the need to always reflect inner truth.

As we move into creating the structures to live our lives authentically, we are in great need of the virtue of courage. This does not mean that we have no fear. It means that despite fear and anxiety, we move ahead. Rollo May tells us that "courage consists not of the absence of fear and anxiety but of the capacity to move ahead even though one is afraid."[28] Letting go of a fixed image of ourselves or of fixed goals and a settled future, moving into the unknown, of getting to know ourselves and come to new goals and new life-styles—these processes are all anxiety producing. We need the courage to accept the anxiety. We can look to no one for approval except the inner Self. Each one must seek approval in his or her own heart. We may have to go through layers of a disapproving self, a guilt-provoking self before we come to the genuine Self, the inner core. Here in our hearts we find approval and courage. Some who will not bear the anxiety and allow their courage to surface will refuse "to move from the familiar to the unfamiliar . . . . They sacrifice their freedom and constrict autonomy and self-awareness . . . . To venture causes anxiety, but not to venture is to lose oneself."[29]

As people move through the mid-life transition period, they cross the bridge into the second half of life with and through the choices and decisions that flow from a new sense of identity and an intuitive sense about the real meaning and purpose of existence. This newborn person (and indeed it is a third birth, a birth into the second half of life) refashions his or her life-style to reflect the reality of who he or she is in every way. Goals and prospects for the future flow from and emerge from the new sense of true identity. Discussing the movement of our civilization into the third wave, Alvin Toffler writes, "The Third Wave is for those who think the human story, far from ending, has only just begun."[30] It is true also of those who experience the third birth, the move into the period of mid-life. They also have a sense that their life is just beginning. The first half of life seems like a preparation for now. They look back to the past and see it all as a progression toward the now moment. Our human story goes on, our becoming continues all through the second half of life.

## Notes

1. Karl Rahner, *The Shape of the Church to Come*, trans. Edward Quinn (New York: Seabury Press, 1974), p. 47.

2. Gen. 37:5, 9.

3. Brian P. Hall, *The Development of Consciousness* (New York: Paulist Press, 1976), p. 39.

4. George Bernard Shaw, "Saint Joan," in *Seven Plays* (New York: Dodd, Mead & Co., 1967), pp. 801-911.

5. Isa. 11:6-9.

6. Rev. 21:1-4.

7. Luci Shaw, "Imagination: That Other Avenue to Truth," in *Christianity Today*, January 2, 1981, p. 33.

8. Gerald O'Collins, "The Imagination of Jesus," in *America*, December 20, 1975, p. 438.

9. Luke 13:34.

10. Matt. 21:1.

11. Luke 6:21.

12. Matt. 12:49-50.

13. Harvey Cox, *The Feast of Fools* (Cambridge: Harvard University Press, 1969), p. 7.

14. Morton T. Kelsey, *The Other Side of Silence* (New York: Paulist Press, 1976), p. 181.

15. Carl Rogers, "Toward a Modern Approach to Values: The Valuing Process in the Mature Person," in *Creativity*, edited by Morton Bloomberg (Conn.: College and University Press, 1973), p. 118.

16. *Ibid.*, p. 121.

17. Eugene T. Gendlin, *Focusing* (New York: Everest House, 1978), p. 158.

18. *Ibid.*, p. 159.

19. Bernard Lonergan, *Method in Theology* (New York: Herder and Herder, 1972), p. 140.

20. *Ibid.*, p. 52.

21. As quoted in B. B. C. television documentary, "The Story of Carl Gustav Jung," produced by Jonathan Stedall, 1971.

22. Harvey Cox, *The Feast of Fools*, p. 222.

23. Daniel J. Levinson, *The Seasons of a Man's Life* (New York: Knopf, 1978), p. 52.

24. Eccl. 3:1-11.

25. Roger L. Gould, *Transformations:* (New York: Simon and Schuster, 1978), p. 44.

26. Harold Rugg, *Imagination* (New York: Harper and Row, 1963), p. 292.

27. Frances C. Vaughan, *Awakening Intuition* (New York: Anchor Press/Doubleday, 1979), p. 169.

28. Rollo May, *The Meaning of Anxiety*, rev. ed. (New York: W. W. Norton and Co., 1977), p. 377.

29. *Ibid.*, p. 392.

30. Alvin Toffler, *The Third Wave* (New York: Bantam Books/ William Morrow & Co., 1980), p. 1.

# Bibliography

Allport, Gordon W. *The Individual and His Religion: A Psychological Interpretation.* New York: MacMillan Publishing, 1950.

Anderson, Joan. *A Year by the Sea: Thoughts of an Unfinished Woman.* New York: Broadway Books, 2000.

Assagioli, Roberto. *Psychosynthesis.* New York: Hobbs, Dorman and Co., 1965.

Baum, Gregory. *Faith and Doctrine.* New York: Paulist Press, 1969.

———. *Religion and Alienation.* New York: Paulist Press, 1975.

Bouwsma, William J. "Christian Adulthood." In *Adulthood.* Edited by Erik H. Erikson. New York: W. W. Norton and Company, 1978.

Bradbury, Wilbur. *The Adult Years.* New York: Time Life Books, 1975.

Buhler, Charlotte. "Meaningfulness of the Biographical Approach." In *Readings in Adult Psychology: Contemporary Perspectives.* Edited by Lawrence R. Allman and Denise T. Jaffe. New York: Harper and Row, 1977.

Campbell, Joseph. *Myths to Live By.* New York: Bantam Books, 1973.

Cargas, Harry James and Bernard Lee, eds. *Religious Experience and Process Theology.* New York: Paulist Press, 1976.

Conn, Walter E., ed. *Conversion.* New York: Alba House, 1978.

Corbett, Lionel. *The Religious Function of the Psyche.* East Sussex, England and Philadelphia: Brunner-Routledge, 2002.

Couturier, Guy P. "Jeremiah." In *The Jerome Biblical Commentary.* Edited by Raymond A. Brown et al. Englewood Cliffs, NJ: Prentice-Hall, 1968.

Cox, Harvey. *The Feast of Fools.* Cambridge: Harvard University Press, 1969.

———. *The Seduction of the Spirit: The Uses and Misuses of People's Religion.* New York: Simon and Schuster, 1973.

De Chardin, Pierre Teilhard. *The Divine Milieu.* New York: Harper and Row, 1960.

De Rosa, Peter. *Jesus Who Became Christ.* Denville, NJ: Dimension Books, 1974.

141

Downs, Tom. *A Journey to Self through Dialogue.* West Mystic, CT: Twenty-Third Publications, 1977.

Edinger, Edward. "Depth Psychology as the New Dispensation: Reflections of Jung's *Answer to Job.*" *Quadrant,* Winter, 1979.

Eliade, Mircea. *Myth and Reality.* Translated by Willard R. Trask. New York: Harper and Row, 1963.

Erikson, Erik. *Childhood and Society.* New York: W. W. Norton, 1963.

Evans, Richard I. *Jung on Elementary Psychology: A Discussion between C. G. Jung and Richard I. Evans.* New York: E. P. Dutton and Co., 1964.

Fiske, Marjorie. *Middle Age: The Prime of Life?* New York: Harper and Row, 1979.

Fowler, James. "Stage Six and the Kingdom of God." *Religious Education* 75:231-248.

———. "Toward a Developmental Perspective on Faith." *Religious Education* 69:207-219.

Fowler, James and Sam Keen. *Life Maps: Conversations on the Journey of Faith.* Edited by Jerome Berryman. Waco, TX: Word Books, 1978.

Fowler, James and Robin Lovin. *Trajectories in Faith.* Nashville: Abingdon, 1980.

Freire, Paulo. *Education for Critical Consciousness.* New York: Continuum, 1980.

Fried, Barbara. *The Middle Age Crisis.* New York: Harper and Row, 1976.

Garry, Michael. *Christology after Auschwitz.* New York: Paulist Press, 1977.

Gelpi, Donald. *Experiencing God—A Theology of Human Emergence.* New York: Paulist Press, 1978.

Gendlin, Eugene T. *Focusing.* New York: Everest House, 1978.

Gerzon, Mark. *Coming into Our Own: Understanding the Adult Metamorphosis.* New York: Delacorte Press, 1992.

Gould, Roger. *Transformations: Growth and Change in Adult Life.* New York: Simon and Schuster, 1978.

Greeley, Andrew M. *Ecstasy: A Way of Knowing.* Englewood Cliffs, NJ: Prentice-Hall, 1979.

Griffin, David. *A Process Christology.* Philadelphia: Westminster Press, 1973.

Guillet, Jacques. *The Consciousness of Jesus.* Translated by Edmond Bonin. New York: Newman Press, 1972.

Hall, Brian. *The Development of Consciousness: A Confluent Theory of Values.* New York: Paulist Press, 1976.

Haught, John F. *Religion and Self-Acceptance.* New York: Paulist Press, 1976.

Heaney, John J. *Psyche and Spirit.* New York: Paulist Press, 1973.

Heschel, Abraham. *Who Is Man?* Stanford: Stanford University Press, 1965.

Hollis, James. *On This Journey We Call Our Life.* Toronto: Inner City Books, 2003.

———. *The Middle Passage.* Toronto: Inner City Books, 1993.

Jacobi, Jolande. *Complex, Archetype, Symbol in the Psychology of C. G. Jung.* Bollingen Series LVII. Translated by Ralph Manheim. Princeton: Princeton University Press, 1959.

Jaffe, Aniela. *The Myth of Meaning.* Translated by R. F. C. Hull. New York: G. P. Putnam's Sons, 1971.

James, William. *The Varieties of Religious Experience.* New York: The New American Library, 1958.

Johnson, Robert. *Owning Your Own Shadow.* San Francisco; Harper & Row, 1991.

Johnston, William. *The Inner Eye of Love.* New York: Harper and Row, 1978.

———. *The Mirror Mind: Spirituality and Transformation.* San Francisco: Harper and Row, 1981.

Jung, Carl G. *Dreams.* Translated by R. F. C. Hull. Princeton: Princeton University Press, 1974.

———. *Four Archetypes: Mother/Rebirt/Spirit/Trickster.* Translated by R. F. C. Hull. Princeton: Princeton University Press, 1971.

———. *Memories, Dreams, Reflections.* Rev. ed. Translated by Richard and Clara Winston, recorded and edited by Aniela Jaffe. New York: Random House, 1961.

———. *Modern Man in Search of a Soul.* Translated by W. S. Dell and Gary F. Baynes. New York: Harcourt, Brace and World, 1933.

———. *Psyche and Symbol: A Selection from the Writings of C. G. Jung.* Edited by Violet S. de Laszlo. New York: Doubleday/Anchor, 1958.

———. *Two Essays on Analytical Psychology, The Collected Works of C. G. Jung,* vol. 7, 2d ed. Translated by R. F. C. Hull. Bollingen Series XX. Princeton: Princeton University Press, 1966.

———. *The Undiscovered Self.* Translated by R. F. C. Hull. New York: The New American Library, 1957.

Kelsey, Morton T. *Adventures Inward: Christian Growth through Personal Journal Writing.* Minneapolis: Augsburg Publishing House, 1980.

———. *The Other Side of Silence: A Guide to Christian Meditation.* New York: Paulist Press, 1976.

———. *Transcend: A Guide to the Spiritual Quest.* New York: Concordia, 1981.

Larsen, Stephen. *The Shaman's Doorway—Opening the Mythic Imagination to Contemporary Consciousness.* New York: Harper and Row, 1976.

Leclercq, Jacques. *This Day Is Ours.* Translated by Dinah Livingstone. Maryknoll, NY: Orbis Books, 1980.

LeShan, Lawrence. *How to Meditate: A Guide to Self-Discovery.* New York: Bantam Books, 1974.

Levinson, Daniel J., Charlotte N. Darrow, Edward B. Klein, Maria H. Levinson, and Braxton McKee. *The Seasons of a Man's Life.* New York: Alfred A. Knopf, 1978.

Lonergan, Bernard. *Method in Theology.* New York: Herder and Herder, 1972.

———. *Philosophy of God and Theology.* Philadelphia: The Westminster Press, 1973.

———. *Theology of Renewal,* vol. 1. New York: Herder and Herder, 1968.

Lynch, William F. *Images of Hope.* Notre Dame: University of Notre Dame Press, 1974.

Mackey, James. *Jesus, the Man and Myth.* New York: Paulist Press, 1979.

Macmurray, John. *The Structure of Religious Experience.* New Haven: Yale University Press, 1936.

Marty, Martin E. *Friendship.* Niles, IL: Argus Communications, 1980.

Maslow, Abraham H. *Religions, Values, and Peak Experiences.* New York: The Viking Press, 1970.

May, Gerald G. *The Open Way: A Meditation Handbook.* New York: Paulist Press, 1977.

May, Rollo. *The Art of Counseling.* Nashville: Abingdon, 1939.

———. *The Courage to Create.* New York: Bantam Books, 1975.

———. *Man's Search for Himself.* New York: The New American Library, 1953.

————. *The Meaning of Anxiety*. New York: W. W. Norton, 1977.

Mayer, Nancy. *The Male Mid-Life Crisis*. New York: Doubleday and Co., 1978.

Mbiti, John S. *The Prayers of African Religion*. Maryknoll, NY: Orbis Books, 1975.

Metz, Johannes. *The Advent of God*. New York: Harper and Row, 1979.

Moltmann, Jurgen. *The Future of Creation*. Philadelphia: Fortress Press, 1979.

Navone, Jonn. *Toward a Theology of Story*. Slough, England: St. Paul Publications, 1977.

Neugarten, Bernice. "Adult Personality: Toward a Psychology of the Life Cycle." In *Readings in Adult Psychology: Contemporary Perspectives*, edited by Lawrence R. Allman and Denise T. Jaffe. New York: Harper and Row, 1977.

Neumann, Erich. *Depth Psychology and a New Ethic*. Translated by Eugene Rolfe. New York: G. P. Putnam's Sons, 1969.

————. *The Origin and History of Consciousness*. Bollingen Series XLII. Translated by R. F. C. Hull. Princeton: Princeton University Press, 1954.

Novak, Michael. *Ascent of the Mountain, Flight of the Dove*. New York: Harper and Row, 1971.

O'Collins, Gerald. "The Imagination of Jesus." *America*, December 20, 1975:437–438.

————. *The Second Journey*. New York: Paulist Press, 1978.

Otto, Rudolf. *The Idea of the Holy*. Translated by John W. Harvey. London: Oxford University Press, 1923.

Progoff, Ira. *At a Journal Workshop*. New York: Dialogue House, 1975.

————. *Depth Psychology and Modern Man*. New York: McGraw-Hill, 1973.

————. *Jung's Psychology and Its Social Meaning*. New York: Anchor Books/Doubleday, 1973.

————. *Jung, Synchronicity and Human Destiny: Non-Causal Dimensions of Human Experience*. New York: Dell, 1973.

————. *The Practice of Process Meditation: The Intensive Journal Way of Spiritual Experience*. New York: Dialogue House Library, 1980.

————. *The Symbolic and the Real*. New York: McGraw-Hill, 1963.

————. *The Well and the Cathedral.* New York: Dialogue House, 1971.

Quenck, Naomi L. *Beside Ourselves: Our Hidden Personality in Everyday Life.* Palo Alto, CA: Consulting Psychologist Press, Inc., 1993.

Rahner, Karl. *Foundations of Christian Faith.* Translated by William V. Cych. New York: The Seabury Press, 1978.

————. *The Shape of the Church to Come.* Translated by Edward Quinn. New York: The Seabury Press, 1974.

Rahner, Karl and Wilhelm Thusing. *A New Christology.* Translated by Verdant Green and David Smith. New York: The Seabury Press, 1980.

Robinson, John A. T. *The Human Face of God.* Philadelphia: Westminster Press, 1973.

Rogers, Carl. "Toward a Modern Approach to Values: The Valuing Process in the Mature Person." In *Creativity.* Edited by Morton Bloomberg. New Haven, CT: College and University Press, 1973.

Rugg, Harold. *Imagination.* New York: Harper and Row, 1963.

Sanford, John A. *The Invisible Partners.* New York: Paulist Press, 1980.

————. *The Kingdom Within.* New York: J. B. Lippincott Company, 1970.

Savary, Louis M. and Margaret Ehlen-Miller. *Mindways: A Guide for Exploring Your Mind.* San Francisco: Harper and Row, 1979.

Schillebeeckx, Edward. *Jesus: An Experiment in Christology.* Translated by Hubert Hoskins. New York: The Seabury Press, 1979.

Schorer, Mark. "The Necessity of Myth," in *Myth and Mythmaking,* edited by Henry A. Murray. New York: George Braziller, 1970.

Shaw, Bernard. "Saint Joan." In *Seven Plays.* New York: Dodd, Mead & Co., 1967.

Shaw, Luci. "Imagination: That Other Avenue to Truth." *Christianity Today,* January 2, 1981:32–33.

Shea, John. *Stories of Faith.* Chicago: Thomas More Press, 1980.

————. *Stories of God.* Chicago: Thomas More Press, 1978.

Singer, June. *Androgyny: The Opposites Within.* Berwick, ME: Nicolas-Hays, 2000.

————. *Boundaries of the Soul.* New York: Doubleday, 1972.

Spoto, Angelo. *Jung's Typology in Perspective*. Wilmette, IL: Chiron Publications, 1995.

Thompson, William M. *Christ and Consciousness*. New York: Paulist Press, 1977.

Tillich, Paul. *The Courage to Be*. New Haven: Yale University Press, 1952.

Toffler, Alvin. *The Third Wave*. New York: Bantam Books/William Morrow and Company, 1979.

Tournier, Paul. *The Seasons of Life*. Richmond: John Knox Press, 1965.

Van Rad, Gerhard. *Old Testament Theology*. Translated by D.M.G. Stalker. New York: Harper and Row, 1962.

Vaughan, Frances E. *Awakening Intuition*. New York: Anchor Press/Doubleday, 1979.

Whitmont, Edward C. "Reassessing Femininity and Masculinity: A Critique of Some Traditional Assumptions." *Quadrant* 13, 1980:109–122.

———. *The Symbolic Quest*. Princeton: Princeton University Press, 1969, 1991.

Wiederkehr, Macrina. *Seasons of Your Heart: Prayers and Reflections*. New York: Harper Collins, 1991.

# Index

# About the Authors

Janice Brewi (right) and Anne Brennan (left) are the founders and directors of Mid-Life Directions, Inc., a not-for-profit organization known nationally and internationally. They have been in the forefront of the contemporary movement of spirituality in adult life and ground breakers in the area of mid-life growth.

For over 20 years, they have facilitated the Mid-Life Directions workshops and retreats for people 35–65+ and Long Life Directions workshops and retreats for people 60–90+. They have also trained an international group of professionals to offer these same programs in their own geographic locations. These Mid-Life Directions Certified Consultants are found across the USA, Canada, and South America, in Ireland, England, Italy, the Philippines, Singapore, Malaysia, Thailand, Australia, Africa, and India. This international character speaks of the archetypal reality of the life cycle and the mid-life experience in diversified cultures. For more information, write to Mid-Life Directions, 4 Palm Ave, Brick, NJ 08723-7222.

Drs. Brewi and Brennan are authors of three other books. All artfully combine the psychology of Carl G. Jung and Judeo-Christian spirituality: *Mid-Life Spirituality and Jungian Archetypes, Mid-Life Directions: Praying, Playing and Other Sources of New Dynamism,* and *Passion for Life: Lifelong Psychological and Spiritual Growth.*

Both Janice Brewi and Anne Brennan have a doctorate (STD) from San Francisco Theological Seminary in adult psychological and spiritual growth. They live and work in New Jersey.